Discussion Starters

Discussion Starters

Speaking Fluency Activities for Advanced ESL/EFL Students

Keith S. Folse

Ann Arbor

THE UNIVERSITY OF MICHIGAN PRESS

This book is dedicated to Tony M. Jones and Jan O. Hamada. That one seldom meets people like these two is unfortunate. That our paths have crossed has been a real blessing to me. They have been extremely encouraging and solid in their support to me not only as a writer but also, and more importantly, as a friend.

Acknowledgments

I would like to thank the teachers who were instrumental in the field-testing of the material in this text at various stages by providing ideas, feedback, and support. In particular, I would like to thank Audrey Blackwell and Debbie Beyea at the University of Southern Mississippi; Carol Mundt at the University of North Carolina at Charlotte; and Patti Heiser, Jim Ward, and Ann Wennerstrom of the University of Washington.

In addition, and in a sign of the times, I would like to thank the many ESL/EFL professionals with whom I have been in touch electronically through TESL-L and TESLMW-L. (For those who do not know of these wonders yet, TESL-L and TESLMW-L are electronic discussion lists available to anyone with a computer and a modem.) In these groups, very special thanks go to David Ross, Anthea Tillyer, Susie Robertshaw, Judee Reel, and Grace Low for their insightful comments and suggestions.

I would also like to thank the staff at the University of Michigan Press who have been instrumental in the completion of this book.

To the Teacher

Teaching Discussion Classes

One of the most challenging teaching situations is the advanced discussion or speaking class. In theory, the teacher (or a student) can bring up a given topic and the students will discuss its merits or controversial aspects. In reality, however, this is rarely the case. In most classes, the most confident students tend to dominate the discussion and the weaker students, those who really need this class, quickly withdraw. In order to keep the "discussion" going, the teacher ends up trying to draw the students out. In effect, this "discussion" often becomes a question and answer exchange between the teacher and a few students.

With a wide variety of engaging topics and unique interactive exercises designed to keep the discussion flowing, *Discussion Starters* aims to balance the speaking loads of all the students in the class and thus promote an environment in which everyone has not only a chance but a real need to speak out. In fact, many times the exercises have been designed so that students cannot complete the speaking task unless everyone in the group participates and speaks up. Therefore, students actually need the input of other students to complete the discussion task.

Using the Book

The most important pedagogical point involved in using this book is that the teacher give the students the time and framework to think about their own ideas so they can form a coherent opinion. It is extremely important to realize that our students have a number of factors working against them: they may lack confidence in their English skills, they may not have any background information about the topic, they may not have participated in group discussions much, they may not be interested in the topic (because they have not been engaged personally), and they may not have any opinion at all about the topic (though this last factor is definitely not limited to nonnative speakers).

These possible limitations of our students have been taken into account, and the exercises within each unit are set up in a special way in order to help the students develop and organize their ideas and thus foster confidence in their knowledge of the topic, which will facilitate speaking. Whenever a question for discussion is introduced, there is a prerequisite exercise which has the students write out their own ideas. This exercise sometimes consists of a series of short questions designed to guide the students through the critical thinking process. At other times, the exercise has two or three questions that are more general in nature but still aim to guide the students so that they can put their ideas down on paper.

This book is built on the premise that having to write out our thoughts on paper forces us to reexamine, rethink, and recycle our ideas until we have a much neater package. At workshops, when teachers are asked their opinion about a topic and then told, before everyone has had a chance to speak out, to write out their opinions in 25 to 50 words, it is usually the case that their written opinions have changed somewhat from their original opinion. Certainly they are more directed and more to the point. When teachers are then asked to continue talking about the topic in question, the discussion seems to flow much better. In addition, teachers who were reluctant to speak up before now do so. The printed word in front of them seems to be an anchor for those who were hesitant or reluctant to speak up before. The simple act of writing out one's thoughts on paper before having to speak does make a real difference in not only the quality but also the quantity (fluency) of the discussion.

For example, when a student is suddenly confronted with the statement "People shouldn't drink and drive," it might be difficult for many students to say something that makes much sense and really expresses their opinion. Most students in this situation in a group will be so nervous about what they are going to say that they can't and don't listen to the other students until after they themselves have spoken. Thus, what ensues more resembles a series of monologues than a dialogue or discussion of sorts. For this class to be a real learning and developing situation with interaction, it is much better (and I would argue necessary) to have the students write out their ideas briefly beforehand.

Topics for Discussion

A quick glance at the table of contents will reveal that the 32 units cover an extremely wide range of topics. Though most of the topics in the text are serious (conservation, gun control, multiculturalism, AIDS), many others deal with lighter topics (humor and culture, group crosswords, traditional fairy tales, unique court cases). The topics that have been chosen do not contain material that will quickly become dated.

Unlike other discussion books on the market today, *Discussion Starters* rarely uses imaginary situations for discussion (e.g., "Imagine that a loved one is hooked up to a life-support system" or "If you could only choose five people to enter a fall-out shelter, which five of these eight people would you choose?") When people have been challenged to come up with a potential solution to a task or problem, they rightfully expect to be able to hear what the "correct" answer is. For example, in the well-known "Baby Jessica" case (unit 6), students are told about the case and then asked to be the judge. After they have discussed each other's verdicts and reasons, they are then instructed to turn to the back of the book to discover the actual decision of the judge or jury in this case.

The activities and tasks in *Discussion Starters* are real situations from all over the world. When students are asked what they would do in a given situation or how a judge should rule in a case, there is a real answer that is provided.

 ## Types of Interaction in the Exercises

Most of the units in this book introduce a problem or controversial topic at the beginning of the unit. This is then followed by a series of exercises designed to prepare all of the students so that they can express their ideas at the next class meeting. A unit usually includes several kinds of oral fluency activities, but some of the major types of activities are listed here.

Problem-solving tasks: A unique feature of this text is that every unit in this text has several tasks in which students must cooperate to solve a problem while using English.

Court cases: Exercises 1.1, 2.2, 2.8, 6.3, 6.6, 6.9, 21.4, 22.4, 24.1, 25.1, 26.15, 28.9, 31.1, 31.10. Each of these exercises pertains to a real court case that involves the topic of the unit. Students are told to work out their own solution as if they were the judge or jury and then discuss their ideas at the next class meeting. Actual decisions are revealed in a special section at the back of the book.

Finish the story: Units 5, 20. A story that has a unique ending has been begun in the unit, but the ending has deliberately been left off. Instructions are given for having students discuss possible endings and reasons for their choices. As with all the material in this text, these are actual stories that, incredible as they may sound, really happened.

Speaking puzzles: Units 11, 29. Students work in threes to complete a puzzle. Each student has access to one-third of the clues. Students must cooperate by giving spoken clues to each other so that they can complete the entire puzzle.

Role-play: Units 16, 19, 23, 24, 27, 30. Though the unit does not revolve around the role-play exercise, these units do include an exercise that has the students do some sort of role-play regarding the topic of the unit. Possible roles are often suggested, but it is up to the teacher to choose which roles should be used. Whether or not role-plays succeed in class depends a lot on the dynamics of the given group of students.

Discussion and oral presentations: Units 3, 7, 10, 13, 18. Though these units contain other types of interaction, one of the main points of these units is that students bring in related material from outside class to present to the rest of the class.

Charts and questionnaires: Units 4, 10, 14, 23, 32. Students must work together to complete information in a chart or questionnaire. Since each student has only a piece of the information in the chart, it is necessary that all students speak up in the activity for the group to be able to complete the chart successfully. Questionnaires actively engage the students at a personal level; later students compare their responses with responses of other students in their groups.

Put the story together: Units 9, 15, 17. Students work in large groups to solve a strip story. Each student has one piece of the story and all students must work together or a solution is impossible.

Small group discussions: Units 3, 8, 12, 18. One of the main features of these units is an exercise that fosters active interaction among the members of a small group (three to five students).

Text Organization

Discussion Starters consists of 32 self-contained units. There is ample background material in the text to start students on their way to a discussion. Teachers do not have to spend time searching for articles that most of the students in the class will be able to comprehend (which is in itself a major job for any teacher), and students do not have to do extensive outside reading in order to feel qualified to talk about the topics. Thus, students can spend their class time speaking about and discussing topics rather than reading about them silently. (Naturally, teachers may assign additional readings to supplement the topics in *Discussion Starters* if they wish.)

An important unique feature of this text is that there are efficient, i.e., simple yet effective, homework exercises in which students must sort out their ideas and opinions before coming to class to discuss or talk about the issues in the textbook. This allows all students to be prepared for the speaking activities in class and is of special importance to the weaker, less confident nonnative speakers. It also allows the teacher to feel confident that all the students in the class, regardless of their native country, education level, or age, now have a known common background about the topic. Some students will naturally know more about certain topics, but now the teacher at least has a common denominator from which to start discussions.

Each unit contains a number of exercises (usually around 10) that provide speaking interaction about a central topic or idea. In most of these activities, students must work together in pairs or small groups to solve a problem, reach a consensus, discuss ideas, or complete some other kind of speaking task.

A particular strength of the design of this text is that there is no set pattern for introducing a topic. Units begin with cartoons, questionnaires, puzzles, court cases, and proverbs. This variety should help keep a discussion course from becoming monotonous or too predictable after a few weeks.

Communication Activities

At the back of this text, there are 55 communication activities. These are an essential part of certain units. In a given exercise in a unit, students are often told to work in pairs or small groups. Student A will be told to look at one communication activity while student B will be told to look at another communication activity. In this way, the students hold different pieces of information which only they know and which they must share verbally with their partner. Since the two pieces of information are not on the same page or even near each other in the text, the students must talk to their partners to complete the given language task.

It is essential that students understand the whole activity before teachers have students do the communication activities. The teacher should give an overview of the exercise, explain how the communication task will work, divide the class into pairs or groups as the exercise says, and then walk around the room to help any students who might still have questions.

Fluency versus Accuracy in Language Learning

All exercises that are done in any language class are done either for accuracy, for fluency, or for a combination of the two. However, we teachers very often tend to do one to the exclusion of the other, and much of what we do, especially what we have traditionally done, is heavily oriented toward accuracy. While this may be appropriate at lower levels of language proficiency, there is a need to balance accuracy exercises with fluency exercises.

For an exercise to be fluency-oriented, the exercise should be slightly below the actual level of the students so that the student can practice extensively without becoming too distracted by difficult or unfamiliar vocabulary and grammatical points. In other words, the students should find the language level in the exercise easy. The purpose of a fluency exercise is to increase the volume of actual language practice that students can accomplish in the given time limitations. Having the students write out their opinions ahead of time, as many of the exercises require, will allow the students to concentrate their efforts in class on actual speaking rather

Comprehensible output → actually speaking

than reading, listening, or vocabulary. Students will learn to speak about a topic in English by doing just that—actually spending class time speaking.

Integrated Skills

Having students write something on the topic before they discuss the topic is innovative and integrates writing and speaking. Although this book is designed primarily to encourage speaking, it calls for other skills such as reading, writing, listening, working in groups, and cooperative learning. Yet this is accomplished without students having to do an extensive amount of outside reading or writing, which allows the students to focus on the primary goal of this text: speaking fluency and discussion skills.

Vocabulary Development

Regardless of any ESL or EFL student's level, vocabulary development is one of the primary concerns of many students. To help students acquire and retain important new vocabulary which pertains to the topics presented in the units of *Discussion Starters*, each unit concludes with a vocabulary check exercise called Language Review. The format for this exercise varies from unit to unit. The seven different formats used for vocabulary review in this text are as follows.

Key word

Read the key word in the left column. Circle the letter of the word that is related to the key word.

    1. maternity   a. importance   b. arithmetic   c. pregnant

Completion requiring some grammatical changes

Use the vocabulary to complete the sentences. Make grammatical changes when necessary.

    expose   hazard   addictive   sue   patch

1. Due to the ____hazardous____ weather around the airport, flights were delayed for 45 minutes.

Dialogue completion requiring some grammatical changes

Use the vocabulary to complete the dialogues. Make grammatical changes when necessary.

    recently   occurred   have to do with

1.   A: Do you want to go to a movie tonight?
      B: The weather's really cold today, isn't it?
      A: Wait, you've lost me. What _does that have to do with_ going to a movie???

Word collocation
Match the words in the columns to form a correct phrase in English.

   _c_   1. abort   a. to do something
   _a_   2. attempt   b. down
   _b_   3. calm   c. the landing

Short answer completion

1. Name two things that hot chocolate and coffee have in common.
   1. Both are drinks. 2. Both have caffeine.
2. What are two things that Colombia and Argentina have in common?
   1. Both are countries in South America. 2. The people speak Spanish.

Definitions

Match the definition from the right column with the correct word from the left column.

       Vocabulary   *Definition*
  _b_   1. patient   a. unexpected, surprising
  _a_   2. ironic   b. a sick person who goes to see the doctor
  _c_   3. in order   c. correct, no problems

Solving problems using the vocabulary

Each question contains an italicized vocabulary item from this unit. Show that you understand the meaning of the italicized item by answering the question.

1. If you have 10 apples, 30 bananas, and 15 potatoes, and if you give 5 of the bananas and 5 of the potatoes to a friend, how many pieces of fruit *are left*?

   _35_

2. If a large *order* of fries can feed two people, how many *orders* of fries does a table of six customers need? _3_

Answer Key

The answers for Language Review, the last exercise in each of the 32 units, are provided at the back of the book. These answers are provided so that students may check their own work. It is supposed that students will use the key only after they have actually completed the exercise. It is further hoped that students will return to the exercise to detect the source of their error to complete the learning process.

Contents

Unit 1

You Can Be the Judge: The New Job

Employee vs. Employer in Wisconsin

Exercise 1.1

Read this court case about a work problem.

In the state of Wisconsin, employers are required by law to provide health benefits during maternity leave and must give returning employees their prior job or an equivalent job in terms of salary and other conditions.

Elizabeth Marquardt was an employee of Kelley Company in Milwaukee. When she returned from maternity leave on December 12, 1988, she found that the company had undergone restructuring and had eliminated her job as a credit manager. Her new job involved supervising one employee instead of four, and unlike her old position, included about 25 percent clerical work. Unsatisfied with the new situation, she resigned on December 13, the very next day.

Marquardt took the company to court. She said that the company had violated Wisconsin state law. Kelley Company defended itself by saying that there was a restructuring and that the subsequent reassignment also took into account Marquardt's long-standing communication problems with customers.

Exercise 1.2

If you were the judge, would you rule in favor of Marquardt or Kelley Company?

_____ Why? Write two or three reasons for your decision.

_____

_____

_____

_____

Exercise 1.3

Work in small groups. Discuss your decision and your reasons. When you finish, read page 173 for the result of this case.

Language Review

Read the key word in the left column. Circle the letter of the word that is related to the key word.

1. maternity	a. importance	b. arithmetic	c. pregnant
2. prior	a. before	b. not public	c. dangerous
3. (take) leave	a. control	b. absent	c. prepare
4. equivalent	a. very easy	b. similar	c. appropriate
5. in terms of	a. requiring	b. concerning	c. demanding
6. eliminate	a. cut down	b. cut up	c. cut out
7. very	a. exact	b. same	c. previous
8. settle	a. solve	b. exit	c. exchange
9. undisclosed	a. wrong	b. secret	c. confusing
10. subsequent	a. following	b. parallel	c. unrelated

Unit 2

Smoking or Nonsmoking?

No smoking anywhere???

Exercise 2.1

Read the following situations and indicate your reaction by circling 1 if you agree strongly, 2 if you agree somewhat, 3 if you are not sure, 4 if you disagree somewhat, and 5 if you disagree strongly. Then write your opinion about these statements. Be sure to include one or two reasons to explain your opinion.

a.   1   2   3   4   5   Smokers should not be allowed to smoke in public places.

_____

_____

_____

b.   1   2   3   4   5   Smoking is one of life's pleasures.

_____

_____

_____

c.   1   2   3   4   5   Smoking relieves stress.

_____

_____

_____

d. 1   2   3   4   5   Smoking should be banned on all flights regardless of the length of the flight. (Remember that some flights last more than 10 hours.)

_____

_____

_____

e. 1   2   3   4   5   Smoking is in the same category as drinking alcohol.

_____

_____

_____

f. 1   2   3   4   5   People have the right to smoke or not smoke. It is an individual liberty.

_____

_____

_____

g. 1   2   3   4   5   The policy of some companies of not hiring someone if s/he is a smoker is acceptable.

_____

_____

_____

h. 1   2   3   4   5   Smoking is hazardous.

_____

_____

_____

i. 1 2 3 4 5 Tobacco companies should be held financially responsible for lung cancer deaths.

_____

_____

_____

j. 1 2 3 4 5 Cigarette taxes are unfair because they are not paid equally by everyone.

_____

_____

_____

Exercise 2.2

Read this court case involving smoking.

> Alfred Deskiewicz, Jr., age 51, of Kirkland, Washington, was a smoker. He decided it was time to quit smoking in 1971. He soon found out, however, that trying to quit smoking is easier said than done.
>
> Mr. Deskiewicz did succeed in quitting smoking years later. However, he had to go to a doctor, wear nicotine patches, and join a health club. The cost of all of this totaled $1,153.54.
>
> In 1993, Mr. Deskiewicz sued Philip Morris, a tobacco company and the maker of Marlboro cigarettes, for this amount. Mr. Deskiewicz contended that Philip Morris had not included labels on its cigarettes which warned that smoking was addictive and could require treatment to quit.
>
> A spokesperson for Philip Morris Company replied that "about 42 million Americans have quit smoking without treatment and 95 percent of them did so without help."

Exercise 2.3

If you were the judge in this case, would you rule in favor of Mr. Deskiewicz or

Philip Morris? _____ Write two or three reasons for your decision.

_____

_____

_____

_____

_____

Exercise 2.4

Work in small groups. Discuss your decision and your reasons. When you finish, read the Court's decision on page 173.

Exercise 2.5

Work in small groups of three or four. Choose *one* of the three sets (A, B, or C) of questions below. As a group, mix up the questions and number them from 1 to 4. Then discuss your answers.

Set A:
____ Do you smoke? If yes, why? If no, why not?
____ Some countries do not allow smoking at all in restaurants. Is this a good policy? Is it fair? Why or why not?
____ Some insurance companies charge smokers higher rates than nonsmokers. Is this fair? Why or why not?
____ If you are a smoker, has someone ever asked you not to smoke? What was your reaction? (If you are a nonsmoker, have you ever asked someone not to smoke? Describe the situation.)

Set B:
____ Why do people start smoking? (First, the nonsmokers in the group should give their ideas. Then the smokers should give their answers.)
____ Is there a real relationship between smoking and a person's health?

____ What do you know about second-hand smoke? What is your reaction to this?
____ If you are a smoker, has someone ever asked you not to smoke? Describe the situation. (If you are a nonsmoker, have you ever asked someone not to smoke? How did you feel doing this? How did the smoker react?)

Set C:
____ Cigarette packages now bear warnings about the potential dangers of smoking. What are some of these warnings? Is this warning system appropriate? Why or why not?
____ What is the biggest reason why a smoker should quit? (If you don't think there is any reason, then rebut the answers that the other members of your group give to this question.)
____ Some insurance companies charge smokers higher rates than nonsmokers. Is this fair? Why or why not?
____ Name places where it is still OK to smoke. Why do you think these places still allow smoking when so many public places have limited or banned it completely?

Exercise 2.6

Smokers should do A and nonsmokers should do B. Write your answers on the lines.

A. 1. There is a lot of pressure in society today on smokers to quit. What do you wish society would consider or keep in mind before it condemns smokers?
   2. Have you ever tried or thought about trying to quit smoking. Did you succeed? Did other people help you? How?

B. 1. There is a lot of pressure in society today on smokers to quit. What do you think nonsmokers should consider before they condemn smokers?
   2. Why do you think a smoker would find quitting smoking difficult? What are some things that you as a non-smoker can do to help a smoker during the difficult time of trying to quit?

1. _____

_____

_____

_____

_____

2. _____

_____

_____

_____

Exercise 2.7

Now work in small groups to discuss the topic of quitting smoking. You may use your answers to exercise 2.6 as a springboard.

Exercise 2.8

Read this court case involving smoking, two divorced parents, and their child.

> Susan Tanner and Steven Masone divorced seven years ago. The wife, Susan, got custody of their daughter, Elysa. Elysa suffers from asthma, a severe breathing condition. Because Steven was worried that Susan's chain smoking was aggravating Elysa's asthma five years ago, he got a court order that barred Susan from smoking in Elysa's presence. However, Susan did not stop smoking around Elysa. After Elysa had an asthma attack one month, a doctor said that Elysa would end up in the emergency room if the smoking did not stop. Steven went back to court.

Exercise 2.9

If you were the judge, what would you do in this case? Give at least two or three

reasons for your answer. _____

_____

_____

_____

_____

Exercise 2.10

Work in pairs or small groups. Compare and discuss your answers to exercise 2.9. Try to agree on one answer (although your decisions may vary of course). When you have finished, read the judge's decision on page 173.

Exercise 2.11

Read each statement and then write your first, immediate reaction. Do not write more than 25 words for each statement.

a. Parents' exposing their children to secondhand smoke is a form of child abuse.

_____

_____

b. A January 1993 study by the Environmental Protection Agency reported that 3,000 Americans die of lung cancer from secondhand smoke.

_____

_____

c. Bill Wordham of the Tobacco Institute trade group said this: "We have to ask ourselves where this [the judge's decision from the case in exercise 2.9] would stop. Is a parent who habitually takes a child to McDonald's or otherwise feeds that child unhealthy food any less deserving of custody? What about a parent who allows his child to watch long hours of television?"

_____

_____

d. John F. Banzhaf III of Action on Smoking and Health (ASH) said this: "Nobody is telling parents they can't smoke. We're simply saying they can't smoke around their children. This is no different from protecting children from lead-based paint or other risks in the home."

_____

_____

Exercise 2.12

Now work in pairs or small groups to compare and discuss your reactions to the statements in exercise 2.11. For which of the four statements did you and your partners have the widest variations in responses?

Language Review

Use the vocabulary to complete the sentences. Make grammatical changes when necessary.

potential	appropriate	condemn	policy	cover
endanger	temporary	custody	suffer from	severe
aggravate	bar	end up	habitually	risk
expose	hazardous	addictive	sue	patch

1. Due to the _____ weather around the airport, flights were delayed for 45 minutes.

2. It's not good to _____ your skin to the sun every day.

3. At first, he only played a few video games, but then the games became _____ and he couldn't stop playing them.

4. Some people disagree with the military's _____ of keeping homosexuals out of the military.

5. In the past, women almost always got _____ of children in a divorce settlement; nowadays, men often prevail.

6. Jan _____ the doctor who mistakenly removed her left kidney instead of her right one.

7. Do you think the teacher's action concerning the student who cheated on the test was _____?

8. Our new insurance policy _____ hospital stays but not dental work.

9. Instead of making things better, I think this medicine has actually _____ my condition.

10. We were supposed to go bowling, but we _____ at the movies instead.

Unit 3

Have You Read a Good Book or Seen a Good Movie Lately?

Exercise 3.1

Work in groups of three. Each student should choose any story that s/he is familiar with. It can be a fairy tale, a short story, a book, or a movie. Try to choose a story that the other members of the group do not know. (Begin by asking them if they know the story that you have chosen. If they know it, then choose another story.) Students will take turns telling the basic plot of their story. Be sure to include the characters and what happens to them. Your time limit per talker is a minimum of two minutes and a maximum of three minutes. One of the other students should be the timekeeper and the other student should be the listener. The listeners will have to report the stories that they hear to other students, so they should listen carefully and ask questions when necessary. Either of the other students may interrupt with questions if something in the story is not clear. Note taking is not permitted.

Exercise 3.2

In the same groups of three from exercise 3.1, students should number themselves 1, 2, or 3. We will now make new groups but in a systematic way. All student number 1s will stay seated in the same place. All student number 2s will move to their right, and number 3s will move to their left. This will produce groups with three new members.

Take turns telling the story that you heard in your original group. Either of the other two students may ask questions for clarification. The teacher will time this activity. Each speaker must speak for at least one minute but no more than two minutes. Keep this in mind as you try to plan the story that you will retell.

Exercise 3.3

Work in small groups. Each student will tell the basic plot of a book or movie that the other students might know. Each student recounts the story until someone can guess the title of the book or movie. Students may ask questions at any time during the talk. Students should not choose rare stories that no one can guess even after the entire story has been told.

Language Review

Use the vocabulary to complete the sentences. Make grammatical changes when necessary.

| plot | character | maximum | familiar with | minimum |
| recount | clarify | clarification | keep in mind | systematic |

1. Could you please _____ what you just said about the final exam questions?

2. I've used computers before, but I'm not very _____ this type of computer.

3. The survivor of the crash began to _____ what took place on flight 882 just before it fell out of the sky.

4. Though the room is quite big, the _____ number of people that it can seat is 85. If you need more space for your meeting, I'm afraid you'll have to use a different location.

5. If you ever need a plumber, please _____. I do very good work, and I'm cheap, too!

6. I like a book that has a very _____ presentation of grammar.

7. The doctor tried to explain what the words on the medical chart meant, but her _____ didn't really help much.

8. I don't like this book because the _____ is too difficult to follow. First, the man gets killed and we think it was his wife, but she's not his wife. Then his sister confesses. Then the man turns up alive. I finally gave up!

9. It's not going to be too cold tonight. The _____ temperature will only be around 50.

10. The most interesting _____ in the whole novel is Margaret. She was wonderful.

Unit 4

Combat Roles in the Military

Exercise 4.1

Finish this story about a soldier who was wounded in battle. Add at least three sentences. Use your imagination to create a unique story.

It was dark, so dark that the soldier couldn't even see the ground. All at once the night sky was filled with explosions of light, and bullets raced by the soldier's ears. A second later the soldier felt a sharp pain.

\
\
\
\
\
\
\
\

Exercise 4.2

Work in small groups (no more than four students). Take turns reading your story endings. When everyone has finished, read the question on page 18.

Exercise 4.3

Step 1. Answer these prediction questions. If you do not know, guess.

> Britain, Canada, Israel, Norway, Russia, the United States

1. Only one of the above countries allows women in every job in the armed forces.

   Which country do you think it is? _____

2. Which of the above countries has the highest percentage of women in active

   duty forces?_____

Step 2. Now look at the chart on page 16. Fill in the names of the six countries. They are arranged in alphabetical order.

Step 3. Information for four of the countries is missing from the far right column, "% Women in Active Duty Forces." The numbers are: 6.0%, 11.5%, 2.4%, and 0.7%. Read the descriptions of women's military roles and then try to guess the correct percentages for the other four countries.

Step 4. Discuss your answers for step 3 with a partner. After you have compared answers and discussed them, check your answers on page 18. What answers are surprising to you? Why?

Exercise 4.4

Should women be allowed to fight in combat? _____ Explain your opinion in writing. Support your answer with at least three reasons.

_____

_____

_____

_____

_____

_____

_____

Country	Women's Military Role	% Women in Active Duty Forces
	Women are allowed in combat jobs in the Navy and Air Force and in all ground forces except in armored and infantry divisions.	
	Women are allowed in all jobs except those in submarines. Future submarines will have separate quarters for females.	**10.9%**
	Women are drafted for military service, but they are banned from combat.	**11.0%**
	Women are allowed in every role.	
	Women are allowed in combat-support and noncombat positions.	
	Women are only allowed in combat-support positions, but this is likely to change in the future.	

Notes: Israel: In the early fight for nationhood in the 1930s and 1940s, women served in combat positions, reaching levels as high as 20 percent of all soldiers. However, the use of women in combat was never formally recognized and was discontinued in 1948. *Russia:* In World War II, women served as machine gunners and snipers and on artillery and tank crews. The air force had three all-women fighter and bomber units. *United States:* In 1991, 35,000 women served in the Persian Gulf war. Five died and two were taken prisoner by Iraq.

Exercise 4.5

Work in small groups. Discuss your answers to exercise 4.4. Try to convince the other students that your opinion is correct.

Language Review

Use the vocabulary to complete the sentences. Make grammatical changes when necessary.

assume	race	all at once	bullet	currently
likely	bar	submarine	quarters	arrange
abuse	execute	bring about	strict	formally
sniper	prisoner	discontinue	P.O.W.	combat

1. The convicted killer was _____ in the electric chair.

2. Cameras used to be _____ from the courtroom, but nowadays we can sometimes see live coverage of a trial on TV.

3. The officers stay in that building, but these _____ are for the regular soldiers.

4. Because rain is _____ for tomorrow, I doubt that we'll get to play tennis.

5. If we had _____ gun laws, perhaps the murder rate would be lower.

6. The janitor _____ all the desks in rows after he had finished mopping the floor.

7. The company _____ that kind of pants due to very poor sales.

8. When the dog appeared at the front gate, the kittens _____ into the bushes.

9. We heard the thunder and _____ the skies opened up. (It began to rain hard.)

10. _____, I'm a student at the local college. However, by next year, I hope to be working for McDonnell-Douglas Corporation.

11. Perhaps it was a gigantic meteor that _____ the demise (complete destruction or end) of the dinosaur.

12. A lingering mystery in the assassination of President Kennedy is the exact number of _____ that were fired. The official conclusion was one, but many disagree with that figure.

Exercise 4.1: Did you use *he* or *she* when you completed the story? The introduction does not say whether the soldier is a man or woman. Why do most people assume that being a soldier is a man's job? This unit discusses the role of women in the armed forces.

Answers for chart, page 16: Britain 6.0%, Norway 2.4%, Russia 0.7%, United States 11.5%.

Unit 5

Finish the Story:
The French Bullet Train

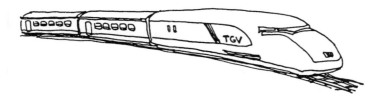

In France, the bullet train is called the TGV. (French: *train à grande vitesse* or train with great speed.)

Exercise 5.1

Read the following true story.

> The TGV is the fastest train in France (and in the whole world). It can reach a speed of 185 miles per hour (300 kilometers per hour). A unique incident occurred recently aboard one of the bullet trains. A passenger was riding the TGV, the French bullet train. When the train arrived at Tours, the police and several specialists met the train. They were there to help the passenger, who could not leave the train on his own.

Exercise 5.2

Think about the situation described in exercise 5.1 and then come up with three possible answers for this question: Why was the passenger unable to leave the train? Write your answers here.

_____

_____

_____

Exercise 5.3

Discuss your answers in small groups. The group should choose its best answer to exercise 5.2 and tell it to the class. Other students should give reasons to prove or disprove the answer or ask questions for further information.

Exercise 5.4

Hot or Cold?

Step 1. A panel of judges should be chosen (perhaps one person per group). The panel should sit in a row of chairs at the front of the room.

Step 2. *Only* the panel members should read communication activity 53 on page 172 to find out the passenger's problem.

Step 3. The groups take turns telling their theories as to what happened. The panel members can only use variations of hot or cold in their answers. Hot means the answer is correct and cold means the answer is wrong.

You're hot.	You're getting hotter.	You're burning up.
You're warm.	You're getting warmer.	
You're cold.	You're getting colder.	You're freezing.

The winner is the first team that can guess exactly what happened to the passenger on the bullet train.

> Useful language:
> Does the man's problem have to do with . . . ?
> Is there any connection between the man's problem and . . . ?
> Was the reason he couldn't leave the train that . . . ?

Language Review

Use the vocabulary to complete the dialogues. Make grammatical changes when necessary.

recently	occurred	have to do with
get/be stuck	get out (of)	on (one's) own

1. A: When was the accident?

    B: It _____ at just past midnight.

2. A: What's wrong?

   B: I have a splinter in my right thumb.

   A: I'll get you some tweezers. Then you ought to be able to _____.

3. A: Do you want to go to a movie tonight?

   B: The weather's really cold today, isn't it?

   A: Wait, you've lost me. What does that _____ going to a movie?

4. A: Do you need any help cooking for the party?

   B: No, but thanks. I think I can manage _____.

5. A: See if you can get this key out of the door.

   B: Sorry, it won't budge. I'm afraid it _____.

6. A: Have you been to Houston _____?

   B: As a matter of fact, I went there on business just last month.

7. A: Was Jack fired because of his attitude?

   B: No, I think the reason _____ his sloppy appearance and bad manners.

8. A: Where's Karen? I thought she was flying home today.

   B: She was, but she _____ in Chicago because of all the snow, so she'll be coming home tomorrow.

Unit 6

Parents and Children: New Family Problems

Exercise 6.1

Perhaps you have seen want ads in the classified section of the newspaper. Can you guess what jobs these ads are for? (The answers are on page 29.)

> Mature Individual wanted to assist in the management of 515 apartments. Must be proficient with IBM PC, filing systems, office equipment. Real estate license preferred. Salary dependent on experience.

> Prepare proposals and assist in development of sales materials for rapidly growing position. Successful candidate will be creative and able to meet deadlines. Experience using W/P and desktop publishing software essential. Ability to organize effectively and work cooperatively as a team member.

Notice a job classified ad lists the skills that the prospective employee should have: must be proficient with IBM PC, must have real estate license, must have experience with desktop publishing software. A job classified ad also lists the qualities that the prospective employee should have: creative, able to meet deadlines, team member. It usually lists expected duties: prepare proposals, assist in development of sales materials, assist in the management of apartments.

For homework, write a classified ad for a parent (mother or father). Be sure to mention the qualities or skills that you are looking for in the ideal candidate for the job as well as the expected duties.

_____

_____

_____

_____

_____

_____

Exercise 6.2

Work in small groups. Take turns reading aloud your classified ad for a parent. Make a list of all the qualifications or requirements that are similar or the same. Afterwards, someone from your group should present your ideas to the class.

Exercise 6.3

Read this story about a child who became famous for a very sad reason.

Cara Clausen was 28 years old and pregnant. On February 8, 1991, her daughter was born. Since Cara had broken up with Dan Schmidt, the baby's real father, she put the name of Scott Seefeldt, the man she was dating then, on the baby's birth certificate. Two days later, Cara gave up her parental rights and allowed her baby to be adopted.

Jan and Robby DeBoer lived in Michigan. Robby had had an infection during her honeymoon and had to have a hysterectomy, which meant she could not have any biological children. The DeBoers were eager to adopt a child, but in Michigan, where private adoptions are not allowed, the DeBoers would have to use a state-approved adoption agency and there was a long waiting period to get a child since the number of parents wanting to adopt outnumbered the children available for adoption by 40 to 1.

The DeBoers heard about Cara through a friend. Though Michigan does not allow private adoptions, Iowa does, so the DeBoers went to Iowa to see about adopting Cara's child. Cara gave up her baby to the DeBoers. In a note, she said, "I know you will treasure her and surround her with love. God Bless and Keep You All." So in February 1991, the baby girl began her life as Jessica DeBoer in Ann Arbor, Michigan.

Later, Cara saw her old boyfriend Dan Schmidt at work and told him everything. She told him that he was the father of the baby she had just given up for adoption. Cara began to have second thoughts and Dan wanted his child back, a child that he had never gotten a chance to know, a child that he had never given up.

The DeBoers were of course shocked to hear that Cara wanted her baby back. They had followed all of the correct procedures and were getting used to their new life as happy parents. The DeBoers decided to fight. The case of "Baby Jessica" went to court.

Cara and Dan Schmidt decided to get married. Cara said that at the time of Jessica's birth, she had not received any counseling about what it really meant to give up her child. (If this adoption had gone through an approved agency, the whole problem might not have happened, since agency adoptions, unlike most private adoptions, require lengthy counseling sessions for both birth parents and adoptive parents.) Cara said she was confused at the time of Jessica's birth. She was a single, working parent in a rural area. Dan said he had never given up his rights as the baby's father. He had never signed away his baby, so it was not right for anyone to take her away.

Jan and Robby DeBoer were convinced that they had followed all the correct procedures. They went to Iowa and brought back their baby. They were the only parents that Jessica had ever known and Jessica developed a psychological bond to them during these two and a half years, not to the Schmidts. The DeBoers also pointed out that Dan Schmidt was an unfit parent because he already had two other children by two other women and he had made no effort to help raise those two children. The DeBoers said that they should not be held liable for the fact that Cara lied about Jessica's father on the birth certificate.

Exercise 6.4

This case was fought over several months in courts in both Iowa and Michigan, the two states involved. Both the Schmidts and the DeBoers won a few of these cases, but in the end one court issued a ruling that the losing party could not challenge. Who do you think Jessica is living with now: the DeBoers or the Schmidts?

_____ Explain your answer. List two or three reasons for your

answer. _____

_____

_____

_____

_____

_____

Exercise 6.5

Now discuss your answers in small groups. When everyone has had a chance to speak, turn to pages 173–74 to find out what happened to Baby Jessica.

Exercise 6.6

Read this story about a girl in Florida who wanted to divorce her parents.

When Kimberly Mays was nine years old, her father Robert told her some terrible news: He and his late wife Barbara were not Kimberly's biological parents. Her biological parents were Ernest and Regina Twigg, who lived in Pennsylvania.

In 1988, the Twiggs' daughter Arlena died of a heart defect. Blood tests revealed that Arlena and Kimberly, who were both born in the same rural hospital in Florida, had been switched at birth. Thus, the girl who died, Arlena, was actually the Mayses' biological daughter and Kimberly was actually the Twiggs' biological daughter.

Once they knew the truth, the Twiggs sought more contact with Kimberly. In a 1989 agreement, the Twiggs agreed not to seek custody of Kimberly in return for visitation rights. After only five visits, Robert called off the visits because they were causing severe emotional distress in the Mayses' home. The Twiggs sued for custody, but they lost in state court. Not wanting to give their daughter up, the Twiggs decided to appeal to a higher court.

Kimberly, who was fourteen at the time, decided enough was enough. She wanted to make the Twiggs leave her alone. She went to court in order to terminate the Twiggs' rights as her natural parents. In effect, she wanted to divorce her parents.

Exercise 6.7

If you were the judge in this case, how would you rule? Why? Give two or three

reasons to support your decision. _____

_____

_____

_____

_____

_____

Exercise 6.8

Now discuss your answers in small groups. Can you agree on what the judge should do? When you have finished, look at the judge's decision on page 174 to find out the final result of this case.

A Mother vs. Her Own Mother in Virginia.

Exercise 6.9

Read this story about a woman who was challenged for custody of her son even though she was a good parent who loved her child.

Sharon Bottoms, who is a lesbian, has one child, a son named Tyler. She lives with her female lover, April Wade, in the state of Virginia. In 1993, Sharon's mother, Kay, asked for custody of two-year-old Tyler. Kay did this because she objected to Sharon's lifestyle. Kay claimed that Sharon's sexual orientation made her an unfit parent. Except for this point, Kay could not prove that Sharon was negligent in any of her duties as a mother. The only issue in this case was Sharon's sexual orientation.

Exercise 6.10

If you were the judge, how would you rule? Who should get custody of Tyler:

his mother Sharon or his grandmother Kay? _____ Give two or

three reasons for your decision. _____

_____

_____

_____

_____

Can you think of one reason that people with the opposite view might have to

support their line of thinking? _____

_____

_____

_____

Extra question for thought: Read your classified advertisement for a parent in exercise 6.1. Did you mention the sexual orientation of the parent as an important qualification in your job description? If not, maybe the parent's sexual orientation is not as important as how well the parent takes care of the child.

Exercise 6.11

Compare and discuss your answers with a partner. When you have finished, look at pages 174–75 to find out what happened to Sharon Bottoms and her child.

Language Review

Read the key word in the left column. Circle the letter of the word that is related to the key word.

1. ideal   a. satisfactory   b. necessary   c. perfect

2. assist   a. attend   b. aid   c. propose

3. proficient   a. available   b. connected   c. skilled

4. deadline   a. calendar   b. travel   c. parents

5. essential   a. prevented   b. required   c. defeated

6. pregnant   a. mother-child   b. teacher-student   c. boss-employee

7. a period of   a. health   b. money   c. time

8. second
   thoughts   a. certain   b. change   c. argue

9. procedure   a. way, method   b. nice, attractive   c. group, association

10. point out   a. increase   b. judge   c. show

11. be liable for a. similar   b. responsible   c. crowded

12. unfit   a. unqualified   b. unannounced   c. unsure

13. give up   a. surrender   b. wander   c. tolerate

14. defect   a. custom   b. answer   c. mistake

15. rural   a. commerce   b. country   c. crowd

16. reveal   a. shrink, decrease   b. create, produce   c. tell, uncover

17. switch   a. admire   b. change   c. swear

18. sought   a. searched   b. encouraged   c. rested

19. call off   a. cancel   b. postpone   c. telephone

20. terminate   a. start   b. continue   c. end

21. object to   a. move   b. disagree   c. correlate

22. grounds   a. ideas   b. reasons   c. samples

23. negligent   a. careless   b. valid   c. emotional

24. an issue   a. cheat, lie   b. build, make   c. discuss, think

25. evidence   a. enjoyment   b. proof   c. occupation

Exercise 6.1: left ad: assistant apartment manager; right ad: marketing administrator.

Unit 7

Proverbs and Values

"Look before you leap."

This proverb means that you should look at something or check it out carefully before you begin to deal with it or work with it. For example, because Victor was going to take all his money out of the bank to buy a piece of land that seemed extremely cheap to him, Maria might say, "Look before you leap! That's all of your savings!" The value being taught is that we should be cautious with a new venture, especially if it involves great risks.

Exercise 7.1

Read the proverbs in *one* of the eight groups and try to guess what the meaning of each proverb is. (Students should not all do the same group.) Then try to decide what value is being taught or emphasized.

Group 1: Don't put off until tomorrow what you can do today.
Too many cooks spoil the broth.

Group 2: Where there's a will, there's a way.
The early bird gets the worm.

Group 3: A bird in the hand is worth two in the bush.
When life gives you lemons, make lemonade.

Group 4: The grass is always greener on the other side of the fence.
Don't put all your eggs in one basket.

Group 5: When in Rome, do as the Romans do.
Don't count your chickens until they've hatched.

Group 6: Don't bite the hand that feeds you.
Don't cry over spilled milk.

Group 7: Haste makes waste.
Every cloud has a silver lining.

Group 8: Two wrongs do not make a right.

An ounce of prevention is worth a pound of cure.

Exercise 7.2

If you need extra help for 7.1, students can read the information in the following communication activities to understand the meanings and usage of their group's proverbs: group 1 can read communication activity 5, group 2 can read communication activity 9, group 3 can read communication activity 14, group 4 can read communication activity 19, group 5 can read communication activity 25, group 6 can read communication activity 34, group 7 can read communication activity 40, and group 8 can read communication activity 46.

Exercise 7.3

For homework, write a situation that illustrates one of the proverbs in this lesson. Write the proverb on the line after the situation.

Situation 1: _____

_____

_____

_____

_____

Proverb: _____

Situation 2: _____

_____

_____

_____

_____

Proverb: _____

Exercise 7.4

Work in small groups (three students is best). Take turns reading your situation aloud (or telling your situation if you can remember all the details). After a person has told the situation, the others should try to guess what the proverb is.

Exercise 7.5

Write down one or two proverbs in your native language. Translate the words (literal translation) and see if anyone from a different language background can guess the meaning of the proverb. Then work with a native speaker to see if you can find an English proverb that expresses the same value as the proverb in your language. (Sometimes the literal translation and the equivalent English proverb will be very similar. However, sometimes they are quite different.)

Your language:_____

Literal translation:_____

English proverb:_____

Language Review

Use the vocabulary to complete the sentences. Make grammatical changes when necessary.

ominous	lay off	haste	content	revenge
premature	fail	close down	accomplish	in charge of
will	put off	spoil	cautious	reply
goal	worm	hatch	broth	calculate

1. If he _____ his driving test one more time, he'll have to wait at least six months before he's eligible to take the test again.

2. The Smiths' new baby was born three weeks _____, but she's doing fine.

3. If you have a strong enough _____ to do something, you can accomplish it.

4. Due to the economic recession, many companies are _____ some employees.

5. Mayonnaise must be kept refrigerated or it will _____.

6. Zina is _____ the accounting department at the hospital.

7. People who are not _____ with their work often complain about even the smallest things.

8. The coach will probably _____ today's practice session until Saturday due to the rain.

9. By the time she was 26, she had _____ more things in her young life than most people do in a whole lifetime.

10. I've heard rumors about the company going bankrupt, but the fact that our paychecks were two days late is certainly a very _____ sign.

Unit 8

Gender Roles in 1850? 1950? 2050?

Exercise 8.1

U.S. secondary schools offer a class called home economics where students learn how to become good parents, sew, cook, etc. Until recently, "home ec" (as it is usually called, much as physical education classes are usually called "P.E.") classes consisted mostly of girls. For example, in 1968, the percentage of boys in home ec classes was only 4.2. In 1993, this percentage had increased to 41.5. What is your opinion of this? Have you ever taken a course like home ec?

_____

_____

Until the 1960s, traditional family roles were that the father go out to work to earn money for the family ("the breadwinner") while the mother stayed home to take care of the house and children ("the homemaker" or "housewife"). Women did not hold a job outside the home and men did not cook or change diapers in the home. Of course nowadays society's concepts of these roles have changed. Write one positive thing (+) and one negative (-) thing about this change.

+ _____

- _____

What is your own opinion about this change? Write it here.

_____

_____

_____

Exercise 8.2

Work with a partner or in a small group. Discuss your answers to the questions in exercise 8.1 for no more than five minutes. Then make new groups and discuss your answers again.

Exercise 8.3

Work in groups of three or four. Read *only one* of these questions and then write your answer on the lines that follow. Make sure that each student in your group does a different question.

1. This unit discusses the changing role of women. Now more than ever, women are working outside the home and the traditional duties such as taking care of the children and the house have been shifted or redistributed. What has this change meant for society in general? Write your thoughts.

2. This unit discusses the changing role of women. Now more than ever, women are working outside the home and the traditional duties such as taking care of the children and the house have been shifted or redistributed. What has this change meant for children in general? Write your thoughts.

3. This unit discusses the changing role of women. Now more than ever, women are working outside the home and the traditional duties such as taking care of the children and the house have been shifted or redistributed. What has this change meant for men in general? Write your thoughts.

4. This unit discusses the changing role of women. Now more than ever, women are working outside the home and the traditional duties such as taking care of the children and the house have been shifted or redistributed. What has this change meant for women in general? Write your thoughts.

_____

_____

_____

_____

_____

Exercise 8.4

Work in groups. Using your thoughts from your answer in exercise 8.3, discuss your answers to these questions:
a. How has the changing role of women affected our world today?
b. Do you think this change has been good or bad?
c. What kind of changes do you imagine by the year 2050?

Language Review

Read the key word in the left column. Circle the letter of the word that is related to the key word.

1. traditional   a. customary   b. obligatory   c. negative

2. earn   a. bread   b. money   c. care

3. consist of   a. need, require   b. search, hunt   c. include, contain

4. mostly   a. very few   b. almost all   c. infinite

5. diaper   a. baby   b. umbrella   c. furniture

6. shift   a. destroy   b. manufacture   c. change

7. breadwinner   a. bakery   b. competition   d. money

Unit 9

Put the Story Together:
The Rough Flight

Can you guess what happened?

Exercise 9.1

Work in groups of nine.* Each student will have a piece of a story. Try to put the story together.

Step 1. Each student should look at *one* of these communication activities: 4, 11, 17, 23, 28, 32, 35, 39, 44.

Step 2. Write your activity number in the box and write your sentence on the line.

Step 3. You have one minute to read and memorize your piece of the story. You do not have to use the exact same words, but you need to express the same idea.

Step 4. The nine students should stand up and try to put themselves (i.e., their pieces of the story) in order by taking turns saying (not reading) their lines aloud.

---

* If there are extra students, these students should be judges and listen to the story lines and decide if the nine students have put themselves in the correct order or not. Conversely, if there are not nine students, the teacher should participate and perhaps one or two of the lines could be copied on a sheet of paper that could be placed on the floor in the correct position within the story. (See step 4.)

Exercise 9.2

For homework, write another strip story like the one in exercise 9.1. Do not have more than 10 lines; fewer lines are OK if you have a smaller class. Try to have a funny or ironic ending. Write one copy of your story on a sheet of paper, and make another copy that you will cut up into strips to pass out to students.

Exercise 9.3

For some reason, it seems that many people are very interested in airplane safety and accidents. Has anyone in your group been on an airplane that had an emergency? Who has flown the most? Who has flown the farthest? Is anyone afraid of flying? Why? (Statistically, automobile travel is more dangerous than jet travel, but travel in small airplanes is statistically more dangerous than travel in motor vehicles.)

Language Review

Match the words in the columns to form a correct phrase in English.

_____ 1. abort   a. what the teacher meant

_____ 2. attempt   b. down

_____ 3. calm   c. rumble

_____ 4. get   d. to do something

_____ 5. loud   e. situation

_____ 6. emergency   f. the landing

_____ 7. ironic   g. ending to a story or joke

Unit 10

Save Our Planet: Is There Hope?

If the planet's in trouble, so are we.

Exercise 10.1

Our planet Earth is in trouble. Every day we hear more and more about the destruction of the environment. Make a list of the three most important problems facing the survival of our planet today.

1. _____

2. _____

3. _____

Exercise 10.2

Work in small groups. Compare and discuss your three most important problems connected to the Earth today. Try to reach a consensus on the top three problems. Then try to think of possible solutions to the problems. Try to suggest realistic solutions. (For example, "not drive cars anymore" is not a realistic solution.)

Exercise 10.3

Read the following three situations. What do you think of them? Are these situations problems or not? Write a sentence or two stating your reaction and any supporting ideas.

a. The world's population reached 5.3 billion in 1990 and is expected to grow by another one billion to reach 6.3 billion by 2000. About 93 percent of this growth will be in the developing countries.

_____

_____

_____

b. The number of living species on earth is estimated at up to 80 million, but only 12.4 million have been briefly described; 25 percent of them are at risk of extinction during the next 20 to 30 years.

_____

_____

_____

c. By the end of the century, the 33 developing countries that are now net exporters of forest products will be reduced to fewer than 10. Remaining reserves of tropical hardwoods in Asia are now only sufficient at current rates of removal to last for about 40 years. The figures for Africa and Latin America are 85 years and 156 years, respectively.

_____

_____

_____

Exercise 10.4

Work in small groups. Compare and then discuss your answers to the questions in exercise 10.3.

Realistically, how long could you survive without a car?

Exercise 10.5

Make a list of things that we can realistically do in our daily lives to help save the planet Earth. For example, "not drive cars anymore" would be great for the environment but is not a very realistic or practical suggestion for most people.

_____   _____

_____   _____

_____   _____

_____   _____

_____   _____

Exercise 10.6

Work with one or two other students. Compare your answers for exercise 10.5. How many of the people in your group actually do the things that have been suggested?

Exercise 10.7

How friendly to the planet are you? Take this test about the environment and you. For each item, write the number of your answer (given in parentheses) on the line.

How Friendly Are You to the Planet?

1. When I have old clothes or old furniture, I usually _____.
   throw them away (3), give them away (1)

2. When I go shopping, I _____ take my own shopping bag to the store.
   always (1), usually (2), sometimes (3), rarely (4), never (5)

3. I usually wash my clothes in _____ water.
   hot (3), warm (2), cold (1)

4. In summer, I _____ run the air conditioner.
   always (5), usually (4), sometimes (3), rarely (2), never (1)

5. My car gets _____ miles per gallon.
   less than 20 (4), 20–25 (3), 25–30 (2), more than 30 (1)

6. I _____ recycle newspapers and magazines.
   always (1), usually (2), sometimes (3), rarely (4), never (5)

7. My refrigerator is _____ three years old.
   less than (1), about (2), more than (3)

8. My main method of transportation is _____.
   walking/biking (1), train (2), subway (2), bus (3), carpool (4), single car (5)

9. I _____ check my car tires to make sure they are properly inflated.
   often (1), occasionally (2), rarely (3), never (4)

10. There _____ a water-saving device in my toilet (such as a plastic bottle which will displace water).
    is (1), is not (3)

---

11. In winter, I set the thermostat _____ than 70°.
    higher than (3), right at (2), lower than (1)

12. I _____ make an effort to buy recycled goods when they are available.
    usually (1), sometimes (2), rarely (3), never (4)

13. I _____ try to recycle glass, plastic, and cans.
    usually (1), sometimes (2), rarely (3), never (4)

14. I usually dry my clothes _____.
    on a clothesline (1), separately (lightweight separate from heavy clothing) in a clothes dryer (2), in a clothes dryer without paying much attention to light weight or heavy (3)

15. Most of the lights in my home are _____.
    fluorescent (1), regular lighting (2)

16. I eat red meat _____ times a week.
    5-7 (3), 3-5 (2), less than 3 (1)

17. When I have leftovers, I _____.
    eat them at another meal (1), throw them out (2)

18. When I drive on highways, I usually drive _____.
    over 65 mph (3), varying speeds (2), 55 mph (1)

19. I _____ use public transportation.
    usually (1), sometimes (2), rarely (3), never (4)

20. In my car, there _____ a bag for trash.
    is (1), is not (2)

Exercise 10.8

Now add up your score for the environmental awareness test in exercise 10.7. Refer to the chart on page 46 to see how friendly you are to the this planet we call home. Discuss your scores and answers in groups. If your score is very high, listen to what students with low scores are doing in their daily lives to help out the environment.

Exercise 10.9

Find a short article on some aspect of the topic of the environment. Read the article and write a summary of 50 to 75 words. Also, write your own reaction/opinion (in 25 words or less) about the information in your article.

Summary (50–75 words):

_____

_____

_____

_____

_____

_____

_____

_____

_____

_____

Opinion (25 words or less):

_____

_____

_____

_____

Exercise 10.10

Oral Presentations

Bring a copy of the article to class and make a presentation to the class. Be prepared to speak between three and five minutes. After your presentation, give your opinion about the article. Other students will ask you questions about the material in your presentation.

(Note: Students should be encouraged to ask the presenters questions. One possible method of doing this is to have students draw names just before the presentation day so that a certain student has to ask the presenter a question. In this way, everyone is required to participate both as speaker and as listener.)

Exercise 10.11

Here are some interesting facts about things we can do in our daily lives and their effects on the planet.

1. Buy the right appliance. The older the appliance, the more energy it needs to run. Replacing your old refrigerator with a high-efficiency type can reduce your energy cost by approximately $70 a year, and cutting our electricity bills helps to reduce pollution.
2. Check to see that your car tires are properly inflated. America could save up to 2 billion gallons of gas per year with properly maintained tires.
3. Drive alone less. Americans drive more than a trillion miles a year, with the average motorist driving 10,100 miles a year and burning up 507 gallons of gasoline. Every gallon of gasoline burned produces 22 pounds of carbon dioxide. Adding just one person to our cars would reduce the number of single-occupant cars and help save more than 33 million gallons of gasoline a day!
4. Bring your own grocery bag to the store. This idea seems so simple that you would not think that it is very important. However, it is. It takes one 15-year-old tree to produce 700 paper grocery bags.
5. Cut down on meat and increase the amount of vegetables and fruit that you eat. It takes seven pounds of grain—usually fertilized corn—to produce a pound of beef; by contrast, it takes only two pounds of grain to produce a pound of chicken. Cows also use up a tremendous amount of water and produce manure and methane gas, which contributes to the greenhouse effect.
6. Putting a plastic bottle in our toilets will not affect the toilet system but will save several hundred gallons of water a year per household in America.
7. Turn off the water when you are brushing your teeth. This could save approximately 300 gallons of water per year per person. In the United States, this would translate roughly into more than 67 billion gallons of water each year ($300 \times 225,000,000 = 67,500,000,000$). Isn't it shocking how such a small thing can have such a tremendous impact?

Language Review

Read the key word in the left column. Circle the letter of the word that is related to the key word.

1. develop   a. surrender   b. grow   c. prepare

2. estimate   a. guess   b. honor   c. pretend

3. up to 10   a. 10 or more   b. about 10   c. 10 or less

4. brief   a. under   b. disliked   c. short

5. at risk   a. in danger   b. on purpose   c. with intent

6. extinction   a. prevention   b. destruction   c. collection

7. remove   a. take away   b. put off   c. add up

8. lasted   a. existed   b. invented   c. saved

9. sufficient   a. productive   b. required   c. enough

10. current   a. knowing   b. present   c. tremendous

11. rate   a. speed, pace   b. effect, result   c. grade, score

12. run   a. contribute   b. operate   c. designate

13. by contrast   a. and   b. so   c. but

14. device   a. instrument   b. awareness   c. separation

15. appliances   a. carpools   b. hardwoods   c. machines

Check your score. The lower your score, the better for the environment. The lowest possible score is 20, and the highest possible score is 70. *Key:* 20–30 = very friendly to the earth; 31–40 = somewhat friendly to the earth; 41–50 = needs improvement; 51–60 = not friendly to the earth; 61–70 = an enemy of the planet.

Unit 11

Group Speaking Puzzle: Movies, People, Food, and Places

Exercise 11.1

Work in groups of three. Student A should look at communication activity 13; student B, 31; and student C, 51.

Step 1: Use the clues in your communication activity to solve the puzzle.

Step 2: When you have used all your clues, ask your partners for clues about the answers you do not know. In this step, students may use the clues in the communication activity, but you may not refer to the communication activity. Try to make up your own descriptions for the words whenever possible.

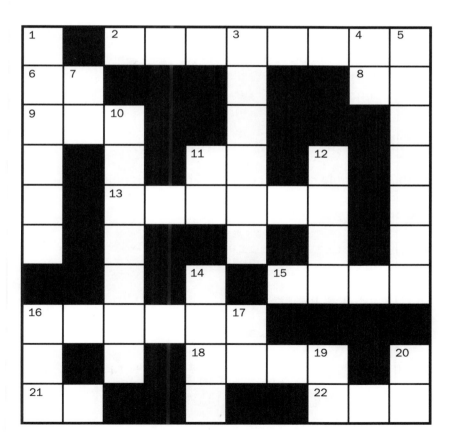

Exercise 11.2

Work in small groups. Discuss your answers to these questions:

a. 12 down is a famous movie (actually, a series of movies). Did you see any of these movies? Did you like them? Why were these movies so popular?

b. 2 across is a famous person. What do you know about her? She was involved in the Falkland Islands crisis (involving Britain and Argentina) and the defense of Kuwait. What is your opinion of these events?

c. 4 down was a very, very popular movie. How many of the students in your class do you think have seen this movie? (Write your guess here: ___. To check your answer, ask all the students in your class.) If someone in your group of three has not seen the movie, tell the basic plot in less than one minute. Why do you think this movie was so popular?

d. How often do you eat number 18 across? When was the last time you ate it? Why do you think this vegetable is not eaten very often?

e. Test your geography. Can your group come up with a list of at least 12 countries that are located in 15 across?

Language Review

Use the vocabulary to complete the sentences. Make grammatical changes when necessary.

planet	preposition	site	okra	continent
jaws	abbreviation	laundry	crisis	geography

1. Words such as *at, in, on,* and *from* are called _____.

2. Of all the household chores, the one I hate most is doing the _____.

3. I've been chewing gum all day. My _____ hurt.

4. It is thought that a _____ used to exist between Europe and the Americas at one time.

5. What is the name of the _____ closest to the sun?

6. _____ is a green vegetable.

7. One of the subjects I always enjoyed in school was _____.

8. Is the _____ for Florida Fla. or Flo.?

9. OPEC's decision to cut oil production in the 1970s led to a fuel _____ in some nations.

10. A mountain in Gunma Prefecture in Japan is the _____ of the worst air crash in that nation's history, an accident in which 522 people perished.

Unit 12

When Cultures Clash:
Multiculturalism and Clothing

Clothing: when cultures collide

Exercise 12.1

Read the following news item about a clothing problem in Canada. Then write your opinion on the lines following the selection.

> Wearing medals he had earned fighting in the British Eighth Army in North Africa in World War II, Pritam Singh Jauhal, a 73-year-old Canadian citizen, marched in a Canadian Veterans Day parade. Later he and five other Sikh veterans were to attend a commemorative gathering at the local Royal Canadian Legion hall in Vancouver. However, when they tried to enter, they were not allowed in because the dress code does not allow headgear and the men were wearing turbans.
>
> Sikhs are a religious group that began in India. For practicing Sikh men, wearing a turban over their uncut hair is a requirement. Thus, because the turban is required, Mr. Jauhal and his colleagues refused to remove their turbans at the legion hall.
>
> Mr. Jauhal stated, "Since we all fought together in the battle against the common enemy, why should we not be able to go like brothers into one room? They are being disgraceful and disgusting." Other Sikhs said that

they heard no objections to their turbans while they were fighting in the wars and wonder why they should hear them now. Furthermore, the Sikhs add that the legion specifically opened its doors to veterans from all countries on Veterans Day.

The other veterans say they are showing respect to Queen Elizabeth II by removing their headgear. In the past, the Queen has met with Sikhs wearing turbans without being offended. Though she is aware of the current problem, Buckingham Palace says that she does not wish to get involved in this particular controversy.

The national Canadian Legion was embarrassed by the bad publicity and quickly issued an order requiring that the 1,750 local branches not consider turbans to be headgear. However, a few local branches have said they will not do so.

_____

_____

_____

_____

_____

_____

Exercise 12.2

In small groups, discuss your responses to exercise 12.1. Do the Sikhs have a right to wear their turbans in the legion hall? Or do you believe that the majority has the right to make certain rules about customs even though it violates someone's religious beliefs?

Exercise 12.3

Read the following news item about a clothing problem in France. Then write your opinion about this situation on the lines following the story.

In France's public school system, no religious expression of any kind is allowed. A recent problem involved several female Muslim students wearing scarves to their primary school in eastern France. The principal of the school suspended the students until they would come to school without their scarves.

The students say that female Muslims are supposed to cover their hair and that their scarves are a religious requirement. The students contend that their suspension is religious discrimination. The government claims that it is not religious discrimination since no religious expression of any kind is allowed in its schools.

(Extra information: One reason that this issue is controversial is that in France there are up to 3 million Muslims, the second largest religious group after Roman Catholicism.)

Exercise 12.4

In small groups, discuss your response to exercise 12.3. Should the girls be allowed to wear their scarves? Why or why not?

Exercise 12.5

Both of these stories deal with a larger issue: multiculturalism. While Canada and America have been settled by immigrants from many different countries, France has not had as large an influx. We often hear about African-Americans, Italian-Americans or Polish-Americans, but France has no tradition of Portuguese-French or Italian-French despite the fact that 7 million Poles, Italians, Russians, Spaniards, and Portuguese immigrated to France between 1880 and 1960.

Jean-Claude Barreau, a government expert on immigration, said "The French are not racists, but they want foreigners to become French, to be discreet about religion, to become integrated at school as individuals. Now, for the first time, we have people born in France who are not French." The situation now is different from that in the past because today's immigrants are neither European nor Christian. The government contends that anything that accents these differences, such as head scarves, segregates the immigrants instead of helping them to assimilate.

In a recent survey in Canada, 41 percent of the participants said they believe that Canadian immigration policy has allowed in "too many people of different races and cultures." Concerning the Sikhs and their turbans, a number of legionnaires have made statements suggesting that Sikhs are somehow less than true Canadians.

Discuss the challenges and problems of a multicultural society. As we move toward "borderless societies," how will the issue of multiculturalism affect us?

Exercise 12.6

Work in pairs or threes. Write a short dialogue (not more than five minutes long) concerning some sort of multicultural problem. Use your imagination—the sky's the limit! When everyone has finished, role play your dialogue in front of the class.

Language Review

Read the key word in the left column. Circle the letter of the word that is related to the key word.

1. march	a. walk	b. attend	c. specify
2. remove	a. take off	b. put back	c. give up
3. refuse	a. out	b. no	c. when
4. respect	a. danger	b. color	c. honor
5. suspend	a. invite	b. expel	c. discover
6. violate	a. a rule	b. a test	c. a wall
7. contend	a. say	b. hear	c. expect
8. integrate	a. activate	b. assimilate	c. participate
9. fought	a. immigrant	b. war	c. clothing
10. influx	a. enter	b. destroy	c. wear
11. segregate	a. tradition	b. enjoy	c. divide
12. assimilate	a. blend	b. affect	c. suspend

Unit 13

Cinderella: An Old Tale in New Times

Exercise 13.1

Can you remember the story of Cinderella? Work with other students to retell the story.

Exercise 13.2

Tell the story of Cinderella again, but change one part of the story. Because of your change, the ending will probably be different. Write your new story here. Begin with the changed part.

_____

_____

_____

_____

_____

_____

_____

_____

_____

Exercise 13.3

Work with a partner or in small groups. Take turns telling your new story. Are any of the new stories similar? If so, how?

Exercise 13.4

Imagine that the main character in Cinderella is not a young woman but rather a young man in a similar situation. He stays at home and does all the work while his stepbrothers enjoy life, etc. How would the story be different if Cinderella were a man?

Exercise 13.5

Work in groups of three. Each student should do *only one* of items A, B, or C below. Do *not* read the other two items. Make sure that everyone in your group reads a different item. Make sure that each student reads *only one* and then writes his or her reaction on the lines following item C.

A. Some people argue that Cinderella is not a good story for children to be learning because of the stereotype portrayed: a woman who is in trouble but is rescued by a man. These people might not like fairy tales because the woman is almost always saved by a man, rarely vice-versa. This teaches young girls that men are superior to women.

B. Some people argue that Cinderella and other fairy tales are not good for young children because the endings are unrealistic, i.e., the endings are always good no matter how difficult the situation is. What do you think about this? Are these good endings in fact bad for children?

C. Some people argue that Cinderella is not a good story for children to be learning because it teaches that beautiful and handsome are good and ugly and poor are bad; in other words, it teaches that outward appearance is a very important aspect in judging a person's worth. What do you think about this?

_____

_____

_____

_____

_____

Exercise 13.6

Work in groups of three to five students. Discuss your answers to exercise 13.5.

Exercise 13.7

    Little Red Riding Hood   Snow White and the Seven Dwarfs
    The Three Little Pigs   Jack and the Beanstalk
    Goldilocks and the Three Bears   Pinocchio

Do you know these children's stories? (If not, have someone else in the class tell the story aloud.) Can you think of things that these stories have in common?

    Choose 2 of the stories: _____ , _____

Make a list of at least 5 similarities between the two stories.

1. _____

_____

2. _____

_____

3. _____

_____

4. _____

_____

5. _____

_____

Exercise 13.8

Make brief oral presentations (two to three minutes) about the similarities between the two stories you have chosen. Listen carefully and ask clarification questions if you do not understand something. After everyone has presented, select the student who had the presentation with the best English (easy to understand), the student who had the presentation with the most interesting (or unique) content, and the student who had the best delivery (spoken clearly and fluently without reading too much and without memorizing the words verbatim). Of course you may add other categories if you wish. Good luck!

Exercise 13.9

Can you think of a children's story that is not listed here? Can you think of any children's stories from your own country? Take turns telling a story that is not listed in this unit. As other people remember, they should be encouraged to add details that they can remember.

Language Review

1. Name two things that hot chocolate and coffee have in common.

   _____

2. What are two things that Colombia and Argentina have in common?

   _____

3. What are two things that your current school and your high school have in common?

   _____

4. Make a list of any new or difficult vocabulary that you found in this unit. Write a brief definition and an example phrase or sentence. Ask your teacher to check your work.

   a. _____ / _____

      _____

   b. _____ / _____

      _____

   c. _____ / _____

      _____

Unit 14

Getting Older: The "Golden Years"?

Can you imagine your 65th birthday?

Exercise 14.1

If you could have any lifestyle you'd like, what kind of life would you want to have when you get old enough to retire from work? (This is usually around age 60 to 65.)

_____

_____

_____

_____

_____

_____

_____

_____

_____

Think of the oldest person you know (or knew) rather well. Describe that person's lifestyle. How old is the person? How is the person's health? Who takes care of the person?

_____

_____

_____

_____

_____

_____

Are there any things you worry about or fear about getting older?

_____

_____

_____

Exercise 14.2

Work in small groups to discuss your answers to the questions in exercise 14.1. Are your answers to the third question similar?

Exercise 14.3

Read these three statements about older people in the United States today. Write *true* on the line if you think the statement is true and *false* if you think the information is not correct.

_____ A 65-year-old today has a 1-in-4 chance of living to age 90. In 1940, the odds were 1 in 14.

_____ About half the middle-aged couples living today have at least two parents who are still living, compared with just 10 percent of couples at the turn of the century.

_____ Two-thirds of all the men and women who ever lived past 65 are alive today.

Exercise 14.4

Compare your answers with a partner. Do you agree on your answers? When you have finished comparing answers, read page 65 for the correct answers.

Exercise 14.5

Have you ever thought about how old you'll live to be? Use this chart to find out how old you might live to be based on recent statistics. Do you know anyone who has "outlived" these expectations?

Life Expectancy Chart

Year Born	Total	Male	Female	Year Born	Total	Male	Female
1940	62.9	60.8	65.2	1970	70.8	67.1	74.7
1950	68.2	65.6	71.1	1980	73.7	70.0	77.5
1960	69.7	66.6	73.1	1990*	75.4	71.8	78.8

Source: Data from National Center for Health Statistics in *The World Almanac & Book of Facts 1994* (Mahwah, NJ: Funk & Wagnalls, 1993).
* Although life expectancy has risen almost every year this century, there was a slight drop that began in 1992. This was due to the increasing number of AIDS cases and deaths from AIDS.

Exercise 14.6

Many people look forward to retirement. However, many others do not want to stop working just because of their chronological age. People are living longer and longer, and many people want to remain productive for many years past the "normal" retirement age. This wish is not always possible due to mandatory retirement age rules.

Question: Is mandatory retirement at a certain age (usually 60 to 65) a good thing? _____.

Write two or three reasons to support your point of view.

_____

_____

_____

_____

_____

_____

_____

_____

Take the opposite point of view. Can you think of one or more arguments to support the opposite view in this issue.

_____

_____

_____

_____

_____

_____

_____

_____

Name three professions where it might matter that the person is over 65._____

_____

Name three professions where it might not matter that the person is over 65._____

_____

Exercise 14.7

Work in small groups. Compare your answers to the questions about mandatory retirement. Each person should state his or her opinion clearly and then give a reason or two to support that opinion.

Exercise 14.8

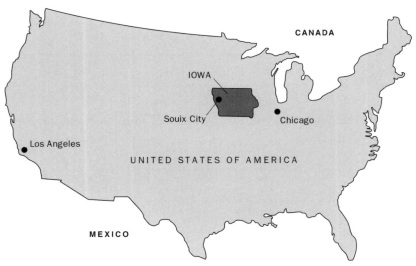

Could a younger pilot have done as well in this crash?

Read the following passage describing a fiery aviation accident in 1989.

FOOD FOR THOUGHT*

On July 19, 1989, United Airlines flight 232 crashed in Sioux City, Iowa. The DC-10 jet left Denver for Chicago without any problems. Midway through the flight, there was a loud explosion, and passengers felt the plane shudder. The captain, 58-year-old Al Haynes, announced over the loud-speaker that the plane had lost an engine (there are three) but everything was fine. Though Captain Haynes had said that everything was all right, the real picture was quite different. Captain Haynes radioed that the entire hydraulic system had stopped working, meaning that he could no longer steer the plane. Though engines go out from time to time, never had a plane's complete hydraulic system gone out. Through a series of skillful maneuvers, Captain Haynes, along with his first officer, second officer, and an off-duty United pilot who happened to be on board, managed to spiral the plane down from 33,000 feet to ground level in the 41 minutes after the

---

*"Food for thought" is an idiom. It means something to think about. Example: I'm not sure if I should move to New York to look for a new job or not, but the chance of getting a good job with a good salary is certainly food for thought.

initial explosion. (The plane could only make right turns, so they flew in wide loops to the right until they were near the ground.)

Just as the plane was about to near the runway, the right wing dipped and the plane somersaulted across the ground, breaking the jumbo jet into large pieces. Amazingly, of the 296 people on board, 186 survived, and many of them were able to walk out of the wreckage on their own through the cracks created by the impact of the crash.

This type of problem had never occurred during a flight. The manual gave no instructions for what to do in this case. In fact, McDonnell-Douglas, which makes the DC-10, had simulated this problem 45 times and not one of the simulations had a successful landing. Safety experts agreed that the high survival rate among the passengers on the ill-fated flight 232 was due to the amazing ability of Captain Haynes to keep the plane under control until the final impact.

On October 31, just two months later, Captain Haynes, with his wife and daughter on board, resumed flying with United. About a year later, Captain Haynes had to retire because he had reached 60, the mandatory retirement age for pilots in the United States. Not even his exemplary flying record was able to gain Captain Haynes a reprieve from the retirement rule.

Exercise 14.9

Now write your opinion about what happened to Captain Haynes. Was it right that

he had to retire? _____ Give two to three reasons for your answer. _____

_____

_____

_____

_____

Exercise 14.10

Work in small groups to discuss your opinions about the Haynes case. Those who agree that Captain Haynes should have retired at age 60 can read communication activity 16 for support. Those who think that Captain Haynes should have been able to continue flying can read communication activity 52 for support. (Rather than have students read more information about a view that they already support, an alternative would be to have students read about the opposite point of view.)

Language Review

Use the vocabulary to complete the sentences. Make grammatical changes when necessary.

initial	somersault	odds	impact	retire
crack	wreckage	dip	manual	simulate
resume	mandatory	steer	stamina	remarkable
entire	take a chance	par	go out	shudder

1. We couldn't believe that he ate the _____ pizza by himself.

2. Classes will _____ at 8 A.M. on the first Monday after New Year's Day.

3. The _____ of the car was so strong that the steering wheel is stuck in the tree.

4. When the landing gear comes down just before landing, you can feel the plane

   _____.

5. In order to get a work visa for some countries, an AIDS test is _____.

6. That child loves to _____ cookies in milk before he eats them.

7. He threw the cup out because it had a _____ in it.

8. I went to the meeting early because I didn't want to _____ that I might not get a seat.

9. Our refrigerator _____ during the night, so the kitchen floor was full of water this morning.

10. No one knows why the ship sank. Investigators are now checking out pieces

    of the _____ from the ship they found floating in the water.

11. Some people believe that eating organ meat will increase your _____.

12. The _____ count of the votes showed Anderson leading Mendez, but by the end of the voting, Mendez was ahead by a mere seven votes.

13. In the United States, many people depend on their Social Security checks after

    they _____.

14. She was the worst student in the class at the beginning of this term, but her

    progress has been truly _____. She is now in the top 10 percent of her class.

15. What are the _____ that two people from the same small town who haven't seen each other in years would go to New York at the same time and stay at the same hotel?

Exercise 14.4: All three statements are true. Some of the information is surprising, but it's all true.

Unit 15

Put the Story Together: The Doctor

Exercise 15.1

Work in groups of six.* Each student will have a piece of a story. Try to put the story together.

Step 1. Each student should look at *one* of these communication activities: 6, 12, 18, 24, 37, 47.

Step 2. Write your activity number in the box and write your sentence on the line.

☐ _____

Step 3. You have one minute to read and memorize your piece of the story. You do not have to use the exact same words, but you need to express the same idea.

Step 4. The six students should stand up and try to put the story in order by taking turns saying (not reading) their lines aloud.

Exercise 15.2

Work in small groups. Write another strip story like the one in exercise 15.1. Try to have a funny or ironic ending.

Language Review

Match the definition from the right column with the correct word from the left column.

Vocabulary	*Definition*
___ 1. patient	a. unexpected
___ 2. ironic	b. let something fall

---

*More than one group can be working on this at the same time. If there are extra (i.e., more than six) students, these students should be judges and listen to the story lines and decide if the six students in the group have put themselves in the correct order or not.

____ 3. in order   c. obese

____ 4. memorize   d. a sick person who goes to the see a doctor

____ 5. take turns   e. learn by rote, learn by heart

____ 6. drop   f. in proper sequence

____ 7. overweight   g. do something one by one

Unit 16

Should Drugs Be Legalized?

Drug abuse is a serious problem today.

Exercise 16.1

All of the activities in the following list involve the use of a drug, but some of these activities are condoned by society while others are not accepted. Read this list of activities involving drugs. Look up unfamiliar words in a dictionary or ask your teacher.

H	DA		H	DA	
__	__	sniffing glue	__	__	drinking a glass of wine with a meal
__	__	taking an aspirin	__	__	smoking marijuana with some friends
__	__	drinking a beer at a party	__	__	smoking a cigarette after dinner
__	__	snorting cocaine	__	__	drinking a cup of coffee in the morning
__	__	taking cough syrup	__	__	shooting heroin

Exercise 16.2

Which of the above activities would you consider harmful to your health? (In the column labeled *H*, put a check b y the activities that you think are harmful.) Which of these activities would you consider to be drug abuse? (In the column labeled *DA*, put a check b y the activities that you think are drug abuse.)

Exercise 16.3

In small groups, discuss your answers to exercise 16.2.

1. What activities do you disagree on as to whether or not they are harmful or drug abuse?
2. As a group, what did you pick as the three most dangerous activities? Why did you choose these activities as the most dangerous?
3. Though alcohol is clearly a dangerous drug, it is tolerated in our society. In fact, many people would not consider it in the same category with the "traditional" dangerous drugs. How can you explain this?

Exercise 16.4

Some people say that drugs should be legalized much the same way as alcohol and tobacco are bought and sold freely. These people believe that doing so would eliminate the underground market for drugs and thus reduce the crime we have in America nowadays. However, many people disagree with the notion of legalizing drugs. Write three (or more) reasons why drugs should not be legalized.

_____

_____

_____

_____

_____

_____

_____

_____

Exercise 16.5

Read this excerpt about the tremendous drug problem in the United States.

Some people strongly believe that drugs should be legalized. These people think that doing so would play a major role in reducing the amount of violent crime that has swept across the United States. Statistics show that many violent crimes are connected in one way or another to drugs: robberies (and murders) to fund drug habits, shootings from turf wars between drug dealers, etc. If drugs were legally bought and sold much as two other drugs, alcohol and tobacco products, this would take the violent drug trade out of the streets.

In 1993, U.S. Surgeon General Joycelyn Elders caused quite a stir when she said that the idea of legalization of drugs should be explored further. She cited the experience of other countries that have legalized drugs and seen reductions in their crime rate. In the same year, Kurt Schmoke, then mayor of Baltimore, publicly stated that drugs ought to be "medicalized." By this, he meant that trained health professionals should be able to give drugs to addicts as part of a treatment program. Baltimore, typical of many large U.S. cities in 1992, had tremendous problems with drug-related crime: 48 percent of Baltimore's homicides were drug related and 60 percent of its new AIDS cases were from intravenous drug use. Unfortunately, these statistics, though several years old, still represent the current situation in many large U.S. cities.

Jails in America are full, and a great number of those incarcerated are in jail because of their involvement with drugs. In the federal prison system, two-thirds of the inmates broke a drug law while only 1 in 10 is in jail for armed robbery and 1 in 100 for white-collar crimes. In 1993, Attorney General Janet Reno expressed concern that the overcrowded jail system was releasing violent offenders such as murderers and rapists to make room for nonviolent drug offenders. She suggested a review of tough mandatory sentences for federal drug offenders, including life imprisonment for growing marijuana plants. Les Hess, chief of the Florida Criminal Intake Bureau, argued against reducing sentences for drug offenders by saying, "If you guarantee that people won't go to jail, there's no threat. Dope is a terrible poison that they're passing off, and it's draining us." While his point has its merits, the bottom line is that "going to jail" would not be an issue if drugs were legalized.

The war on drugs that the U.S. government has waged for so many years is being lost all across this country. The main focus of this war on drugs, stopping the supply of drugs, has had very limited success. Statistics show that drugs are just as readily available today in most cities across the United States as they were when then President Reagan launched his war on drugs in 1981. The total cost of this government-led war on drugs has run more than $100 billion. Each year the Coast Guard spends countless millions of dollars trying to keep drugs out, but for every boat or plane that is caught with illegal drugs, many more get in. The geography of the United States, with its 12,383-mile (19,929-km) coastline, does not favor keeping out illegal drugs. There have been many attempts to get poor growers in South American countries such as Colombia and Bolivia to cut down on the amount of drug-producing crops grown there, but these programs have met with mediocre success at best.

Clearly, the situation in the United States is not getting any better. In fact, for the average citizen, fearful of crime, perhaps it is time to change the situation by legalizing drugs.

Exercise 16.6

What is your opinion about this matter? Should drugs be legalized? _____

Write three or four sentences to explain your answer. _____

_____

_____

_____

_____

_____

_____

_____

Exercise 16.7

Work in small groups. Discuss your answers and opinions about this question: Should drugs be legalized? What are the benefits? What are the dangers? What is the overall consensus of your group?

Though a common sight in society, alcohol is a powerful, addictive drug.

Exercise 16.8

Today alcohol is sold in most areas of the United States, but some counties, known as "dry counties," do not allow the sale of alcohol at any time. Though this prohibition of selling alcohol is restricted to just a few places nowadays, at one time liquor was prohibited throughout the United States. Read this passage about this era in American history commonly referred to as Prohibition.

Prohibition was an effort to stop people from drinking alcohol in the United States. Though there were many attempts at introducing prohibition laws in the 1800s, Prohibition did not take effect nationwide until 1920, when an amendment to the Constitution expressly prohibiting the manufacture or sale of alcohol was ratified. At first, Prohibition was largely successful. However, people soon became divided on the issue. Prohibition was favored by the mostly Protestant settlers whose families had lived in the United States for at least one generation. They believed that drinking was a threat to law and order in the big cities where most of the newly arrived immigrants lived, often in depressing and difficult situations. These people, most of whom lived in the rural country area, did not have any traditions with alcohol. However, the newly arrived immigrants, who were mostly Catholic or Jewish, were accustomed by their traditions to some kind of alcohol. The Irish drank whiskey or beer, the Italians, Greeks, and Jews drank wine, and the Germans and Poles drank beer. These people could not understand why something that they and their ancestors had always done was now taboo.

Though many people followed the law concerning alcohol, mainly because of the $1,000 fine or six-month jail sentence, the first of many daring alcohol thefts took place in Chicago when six masked men broke into a railroad yard and stole $100,000 worth of alcohol. This marked the rise of the legendary gangsters who grew into what is known today as the Mafia. People became more and more curious about alcohol, and people who never drank were drinking. In fact, by the late 1920s, there were more speakeasys, illegal bars, than there ever were saloons before Prohibition.

In 1933, the 21st Amendment to the Constitution officially ended this tragic era of American history. This end came about because it was acknowledged that Prohibition had failed. Despite its seemingly good intentions, Prohibition had increased lawlessness and drinking and had actually increased alcohol abuse.

Exercise 16.9

Has this affected your opinion about legalizing drugs? Why or why not? Write two or three sentences to explain your answer.

_____

_____

_____

_____

_____

_____

Exercise 16.10

Work in small groups. Discuss your answers and opinions about the question of whether drugs should be legalized. What, if anything, should we have learned from Prohibition?

Exercise 16.11

Role-Play

Scene: Several people at a dinner party are discussing whether or not drugs should be legalized. Possible participants: an average citizen, a parent, a police officer, a person who was robbed (possibly for drug money), a person who likes to smoke a little marijuana occasionally, a former heroin addict, a resident in an area with a lot of drug deals on the streets.

Your role: _____

Your position on this issue: _____

_____

_____

_____

_____

_____

Language Review

Use the vocabulary to complete the sentences. Make grammatical changes when necessary.

condone	eliminate	underground	play a role	fund
cite	typical	homicide	cause a stir	inmate
readily	launch	cut down on	the bottom line	restrict
era	expressly	generation	take effect	sentence
fine	threat	break into	come about	taboo

1. The judgment will be a five-month _____ and/or a $4,000 _____.

2. To put it as simply as possible, the aim of the new anti-smoking law is to

    _____ or _____ smoking.

3. The presenter last night _____ many solid statistics to support her point.

4. The wide availability of handguns certainly _____ in the rising num-

   ber of _____ in the state this year.

5. A _____ family in America during that particular _____ consisted of two parents, six children, and one to two grandparents.

6. A thief _____ the museum during the night and stole 14 paintings.

7. For any business, _____ is profit: no profit, no business.

8. Goodson's Furniture Store is _____ a promotion of their new line of
   furniture.

Unit 17

Put the Story Together: The Truck Driver

Can you guess what happened?

Exercise 17.1

Work in groups of 10.* Each student will have a piece of a story. Try to put the story together.

Step 1. Each student should look at *one* of these communication activities: 3, 8, 15, 22, 29, 36, 41, 45, 49, 55.

Step 2. Write your activity number in the box and write your sentence on the line.

☐ _____

---

*If there are extra students, these students should be judges and listen to the story lines and decide if the 10 students have put themselves in the correct order or not. Conversely, if there are not 10 students, the teacher should participate and perhaps one or two of the lines could be copied on a sheet of paper that could be placed on the floor in the correct position within the story.

Step 3. You have one minute to read and memorize your piece of the story. You do not have to use the exact same words, but you need to express the same idea.

Step 4. The 10 students should stand up and try to put themselves (i.e., their pieces of the story) in order by taking turns saying (not reading) their lines aloud.

Exercise 17.2

Work in small groups. Write another strip story like the one in exercise 17.1. Try to have a funny or ironic ending.

Language Review

Each question contains an italicized vocabulary item from this unit. Show that you understand the meaning of the italicized item by answering the question.

1. If you have 10 apples, 30 bananas, and 15 potatoes, and if you give 5 of the bananas and 5 of the potatoes to a friend, how many pieces of fruit *are left?*

   _____

2. If a large *order* of fries can feed two people, how many *orders* of fries does a table of six customers need? _____

3. What are some kinds of food that we peel but are *tough* to peel without a knife?

   _____

4. While driving, have you ever *run over* an animal? What kind of animal was it? Tell what happened and what you did afterwards. _____

   _____

   _____

   _____

5. What was the last food that you *couldn't help* eating a lot of? Where did you eat it? _____

Unit 18

Is It Funny? Culture and Humor

Exercise 18.1

Look at the two cartoons. What is your reaction to the cartoons? Answer the questions about the cartoons.

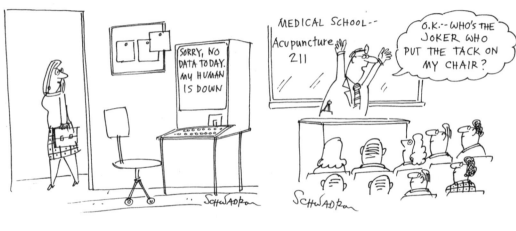

Cartoon A   Cartoon B

Briefly describe what is happening in cartoon A. _____

_____

Is cartoon A funny? _____ Why or why not? _____

_____

_____

Now briefly describe what is happening in cartoon B. _____

_____

Is cartoon B funny? _____ Why or why not? _____

_____

_____

_____

Which of the cartoons is funnier to you? _____ Why do you think this is so?

_____

_____

_____

Exercise 18.2

Work in small groups. Discuss your answers to the general question of what is funny and what is not funny. Which of the cartoons is thought to be funnier—A or B? What reasons do the members of your group have for their decisions?

Exercise 18.3

Read the cartoons in a newspaper. Cut out one that you like and bring it to class. Take turns presenting your cartoons to the rest of the class. Discuss which ones are the funniest and why. Are there some cartoons that some nationalities find funny but others do not?

Exercise 18.4

Read these five jokes. Rank them from 1 to 5, with 1 being the funniest and 5 being the least funny.

____ A mother mouse was outside with her three baby mice. Suddenly a hungry cat appeared in front of them. The little babies were afraid for their lives, but the mother mouse wasn't. She turned to the cat, looked him directly in the eyes, and shouted, "Bow wow. Woof woof!" The cat turned and ran away. The mother then said to her children, "You see. It pays to be able to speak another language."

_____ A woman was on a flight from Miami to Denver. She had not flown very much, so she was sort of nervous during the flight. Everything went smoothly— a good takeoff, no turbulence during the flight, and a soft landing. As she was getting off the plane, the captain was standing near the doorway talking to some of the passengers. When she got near the captain, the woman smiled and said, "Nice flight. How long have you been flying?" The pilot suddenly got a worried look on his face and asked, "You mean including today?"

_____ A woman went into a small restaurant. She looked at the menu and chose what she wanted to eat. The waiter noticed that she had closed her menu, so he came over to the table. "May I take your order now?" he asked. "Yes," she said, "I'd like a steak that is burned on the outside, french fries that are so greasy that they stick together, and for dessert a piece of chocolate cake that is as hard as a rock." The waiter was shocked and said, "Ma'am, we can't do that." The lady smiled and said, "I don't see why not. You did it the last time I came in here."

_____ A man went to a pizza restaurant by himself. The waitress said, "May I take your order?" "Yes," he began, "I'll have the extra large pizza." The waitress was a bit surprised because the extra large is enough pizza for three to four people, but this guy was alone. "Would you like that cut into six to eight slices?" she asked. The man thought about it for a moment and then said, "You'd better cut it into six pieces. I don't think I can eat eight."

_____ A man and woman were having dinner in a restaurant when another woman suddenly came up to the table and said, "You're Nancy Lee, aren't you? I used to live down the street from you." The woman at the table said, "Yes, that's right." The other woman said, "You look terrible. Have you been in the hospital recently?" Nancy answered, "No, I haven't. Now I remember you. You're Victoria Newson. You've gained so much weight that I didn't recognize you at first." Victoria was embarrassed, said a nice good-bye, and left the table. Mr. Lee said to his wife, "I'm surprised you didn't get angry when Victoria said you looked as if you had been in the hospital." Nancy replied, "I don't get angry. I get even."

Exercise 18.5

Work in groups. Discuss your answers to exercise 18.4. Which two jokes were chosen as the funniest by the people in your group? What makes these two jokes funny? Why are the other jokes not so funny?

Exercise 18.6

Can you think of a joke in your native language? Write the joke out in English. Then take turns sharing your joke with the rest of the class. Do not use jokes with foul language or inappropriate content.

_____

_____

_____

_____

_____

_____

_____

_____

Exercise 18.7

Ask a native speaker to tell you a joke. (You could also consult a magazine or book that has jokes if you cannot talk to a native speaker.) Write down the joke here. At the next class meeting, take turns telling (not reading) your joke to the rest of the class. Practice ahead of time so you can deliver the punch line correctly.

_____

_____

_____

_____

_____

_____

_____

_____

Language Review

Read the key word in the left column. Circle the letter of the word that is related to the key word.

1. foul   a. language   b. beliefs   c. furniture

2. content   a. of a book   b. of an author   c. of a title

3. sort of   a. therefore   b. occasionally   c. somewhat

4. turbulence   a. on a picnic   b. on a flight   c. on a bill

5. be down   a. by accident   b. out of order   c. under control

6. brief   a. long   b. none   c. short

7. used to live a. have lived   b. is living   c. lived

8. reply   a. look like   b. do again   c. answer

9. get even   a. recover   b. revenge   c. review

10. stick   a. raise, increase   b. attach, connect c. examine, inspect

Unit 19

AIDS: A Global Crisis

Almost everyone today recognizes the red ribbon
as a symbol of the fight against AIDS.

Exercise 19.1

Read the following situations and indicate your reaction by circling 1 if you agree strongly, 2 if you agree somewhat, 3 if you are not sure, 4 if you disagree somewhat, and 5 if you disagree strongly. Then write your opinion about these statements. Be sure to include one or two reasons to explain your opinion.

a. 1   2   3   4   5   Health workers such as dentists and doctors should have to be tested for AIDS.

_____

_____

b. 1   2   3   4   5   Schools should have sex education programs that teach how AIDS is spread.

_____

_____

c. 1   2   3   4   5   Government health programs need to promote the use of condoms through the media (TV, radio, newspapers, magazines).

_____

_____

d.   1   2   3   4   5   AIDS is a gay disease.

_____

_____

e.   1   2   3   4   5   Schools should have condom machines in the restrooms.

_____

_____

f.   1   2   3   4   5   The government should set up needle exchange programs for drug addicts.

_____

_____

g.   1   2   3   4   5   People who contract AIDS deserve what they get.

_____

_____

h.   1   2   3   4   5   Countries should require tourists to pass an AIDS test before they can get a visa to enter the country.

_____

_____

Exercise 19.2

Work in small groups. Discuss your opinions and supporting reasons from exercise 19.1.

Exercise 19.3

How is having AIDS different for the victim than having cancer or other serious diseases? What special kinds of problems do AIDS victims encounter?

_____

_____

_____

_____

_____

_____

_____

Exercise 19.4

In small groups, discuss your answers and opinions given in exercise 19.3.

People with AIDs cannot marry in Utah.

Exercise 19.5

Since 1987, the state of Utah has had a law that bans marriages if either person has the AIDS virus. In 1993, five people sued to overturn this state law on the grounds that it violates the 1990 federal Americans with Disabilities Act. Do you think it is

OK to ban marriages if one partner has the AIDS virus? _____

Write your opinion about this situation. _____

_____

_____

_____

_____

Now take the opposing view. Write one or two reasons that people might have for

disagreeing with what you have written above. _____

_____

_____

_____

_____

Exercise 19.6

In small groups, discuss your answers and opinions given in exercise 19.5. What is
the consensus of your group? Was the Utah State action appropriate?

Exercise 19.7

AIDS Deaths and New AIDS Cases in the U.S., 1988–94					
	All Years	1988	1990	1992	1994
Deaths	284,249	21,019	31,339	40,072	44,052
New cases	410,532	35,662	48,092	75,908	58,255

Source: Data from National Center for Health Statistics, in *The World Almanac & Book of Facts 1996*
(Mahwah, NJ: Funk & Wagnalls, 1995).

The only immediate hope for containing this epidemic is a stronger emphasis on
prevention, stopping the spread of this disease, since a cure appears to be a distant
reality. Unfortunately, this line of action demands a constant uphill battle that often
results in small gains in areas that are often quite controversial: better sex education, promotion of condoms, needle exchange programs for drug addicts, safer
blood supplies, and improved treatment of venereal diseases that increase the
chances of the spread of AIDS.

Project: A city with a population of 400,000 has just set aside $110,000 of its annual budget for AIDS prevention. The city wants to increase AIDS awareness. Work with other students to come up with ways the city can spend this money in the most effective manner.

_____

_____

_____

_____

_____

_____

_____

_____

Exercise 19.8

Take turns making presentations of your ideas to the rest of the class. After all the presentations are finished, as a class choose the best five ideas. (After you have finished your discussion and have chosen the best five ideas, read the questions on page 89 for some extremely important information about this project.)

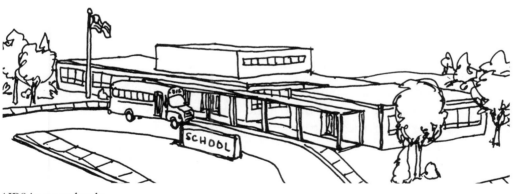

AIDS in our schools

Exercise 19.9

Should a child who is HIV-positive (this means the child has been exposed to AIDS and can pass it on to someone else through exchange of body fluids but has not developed AIDS yet) be allowed to attend public school? _____

Explain your answer in 75–125 words. _____

_____

_____

_____

_____

_____

_____

_____

_____

_____

Exercise 19.10

Work in small groups. Take turns answering the question whether or not children who are HIV-positive should be allowed to go to public schools. What is your group's general consensus?

Exercise 19.11

Role-Play

Situation: Parent A wants to enroll his daughter who is HIV-positive in the local elementary school, but some of the parents have complained that this is too dangerous. Possible roles: the child's mother and/or father, two or three students in the class, the parents of some of the other kids, doctor, school principal.

Your role: _____

Your position on this issue: _____

_____

_____

_____

Language Review

Use the vocabulary to complete the sentences. Make grammatical changes when necessary.

emphasis	spread	contact	come up with	expose
effective	violate	overturn	controversial	set up
exchange	deserve	persistent	awareness	fluid

1. The principal _____ a special schedule for the students who needed extra help with reading and writing.

2. Don't give up. Be _____. One day you'll achieve your goals.

3. Many grammar books _____ verbs because students need a lot of practice with them.

4. I _____ the medium shirt for a larger one.

5. The most common body _____ is blood.

6. He _____ a serious law and was deported from that country.

7. The teacher wanted us to _____ two solutions to the first math problem, but we couldn't.

8. The teacher gave her an 82 on the composition, but she thought she

   _____ a higher score.

9. A cold can _____ quite easily from person to person.

10. One of the most _____ ways to improve your English is to watch T.V.

Exercise 19.7, 19.8: This project deals with an annual AIDS prevention budget of $110,000 for a city with a population of 400,000. Does this seem like enough money for such an important issue? What is the population of the city where you currently live? What is the annual AIDS budget for that city? How many people have died from AIDS in this city in the last year? How many cases of HIV were reported last week? (This information can sometimes be found in the local newspaper.) It is likely that you will find that the budget for this dreaded disease, which continues to spread and kill, is very, very small.

Unit 20

Finish the Story: The Math Test

MATH TEST

Name: _____

Date: _____

1. $45 + 82 =$ _____
2. $88 - 14 =$ _____
3. $75 \times 3 =$ _____
4. $\frac{1}{2} + \frac{2}{3} =$ _____
5. $100 - 58 =$ _____
6. $88/4 - 1 =$ _____
7. $2e + 20 = 40$; $e =$ _____
8. $(x + 4)(x - 4) = 97$; $x =$ _____
9. $56 - 16 =$ _____

Can you guess what happened?

Exercise 20.1

Read the following true story.

    Janice Burke is a math teacher in Mesa, Arizona. When she was giving a test to her fifth-grade class one day, something unexpected happened. This occurrence was so strange that it interrupted the math test. The teacher is OK now, and so are the students. However, when asked about this occurrence, one of the pupils, 10-year-old Jamie Morgan, said, "We got real scared."

Exercise 20.2

Work in small groups. Come up with three possible answers for this question: What was the occurrence that interrupted the math class? Write your three answers in the spaces below. Circle the number of the most likely explanation.

1. _____

2. _____

3. _____

Exercise 20.3

As a class, each group should choose its best answer from exercise 20.2 and tell it to the class. Be ready to give reasons to support your answers.

When another group presents their answers, ask questions or give facts in order to show why their answers are not likely to be correct.

Exercise 20.4

Guessing Game

Step 1. Two to four students should be the "wise people with all the answers." They should sit in front of the class. *Only these students* should read communication activity 43 to find out what really happened in the math class.

Step 2. The other students should divide into teams and take turns asking questions about the situation.

Step 3. The "wise students" should give answers (and hints if needed) until one of the teams can guess what really happened in the math class.

Language Review

Each question contains an italicized vocabulary item from this unit. Show that you understand the meaning of the italicized item by answering the question.

1. Have you ever seen or heard a woman having *labor pains?* _____ Was it in real life or just on television or a movie? _____ Describe what you saw and heard. _____

_____

_____

_____

2. If Mr. Hanks is the regular teacher and Mr. Chavez is the *substitute*, what is the

    name of the teacher who fills in when the teacher is sick? _____

3. Name a kind of food that *obviously* takes very little time to prepare.

    _____

4. What is the most important traffic notice to *pay attention to?*

    _____

5. What are three places where you might find an *intercom?* _____,

    _____, _____

6. Write two other new vocabulary words and meanings.

    (a) _____: _____

        _____

    (b) _____: _____

        _____

Unit 21

Gun Control

What's the future of guns and gun control in the United States?

Exercise 21.1

Answer these questions about guns.

1. Do you have a gun in your home now? _____ Have you ever lived in

   a house where there was a gun? _____

2. Have you ever seen a gun (in real life—not just on T.V.)? _____

3. Have you ever held a gun in your own hands? _____

4. Have you ever fired a gun? _____ If yes, why did you fire the gun?

   _____

5. Have you ever killed an animal with a gun? _____ If yes, what kind of

   animal did you kill and why did you kill it? _____

   _____

6. Have you ever seen someone get shot (in real life—not just on T.V.)? _____

   If yes, describe the situation. _____

   _____

_____

_____

7. What do you know about guns in the United States? Write down as many things

    as possible. _____

    _____

    _____

    _____

    _____

    _____

    _____

Exercise 21.2

Work in groups. Discuss the topic of guns using the questions from exercise 21.1. Finish your discussion with this question: Do you believe that guns are a problem in the United States?

Exercise 21.3

Many Americans feel they have the right to have a gun according to the Bill of Rights (the first ten amendments attached to the U.S. Constitution). The Second Amendment reads: "A well-regulated militia, being necessary to the security of a free state, the right of the people to keep and bear arms shall not be infringed."

Compare this situation with those in other countries. Can people in your country own guns? Do most people own a gun? Why or why not? What percentage of American homes have at least one gun? (Check page 99 for the correct answer.)

_____

An international tragedy: Is owning a gun a right?

Exercise 21.4

In 1992, a sad case which revealed the stark differences among different nations' attitudes toward guns took place in the United States. Read this excerpt, which describes what happened.

In October 1992, Yoshihiro Hattori, an energetic, outgoing 16-year-old exchange student from Japan, went to a Halloween party with his American host, Webb Haymaker, in Baton Rouge, Louisiana. Since they were going to a Halloween costume party, the two were dressed in costumes. Unfortunately, they mistook the house number and by mistake went to a nearby house, inhabited by Rodney Peairs, his wife Bonnie, and their young baby. Yoshihiro and Webb frightened Mrs. Peairs, who called for her husband to get his gun. Mr. Peairs said that he thought Yoshihiro was an intruder. Though Mr. Peairs shouted "Freeze," Yoshihiro, who did not speak much English, did not stop walking toward the house. He said, "I'm here for the party," and was jumping in the air, trying to imitate John Travolta, the character that he was dressed up as. Mr. Peairs fired his gun, killing Yoshihiro.

Mr. Peairs was taken into custody and released that same night because "there was no criminal intent." A 1976 Louisiana law says that a homeowner is justified in killing intruders if he "reasonably" believes that his life is in danger or that the shooting will prevent a break-in. (Someone had previously stolen the Peairs' truck from their driveway; it was never recovered.)

Exercise 21.5

The Hattori case went to court shortly afterward. Rodney Peairs faced a charge of manslaughter, the unlawful killing of someone without premeditation. If you were

on the jury, how would you rule (guilty or not guilty)? _____

In the state of Louisiana, the maximum penalty for this would be 40 years in jail.

What sentence would you hand down? _____

_____

Write two or three reasons for your decision. _____

_____

_____

_____

_____

Exercise 21.6

Work in small groups. Discuss your decision and your reasons. When you finish, read the jury's decision on page 175.

Exercise 21.7

Many people believe that the solution to the increasing number of deaths from guns is gun control. This could mean that the average citizen would not be allowed to own or possess a gun. Although many people support this idea, many others are against it. Work in groups of four to six people. Each students should do *one* of these communication activities: 2, 10, 20, 26, 38, 50.

Write your position on this issue: _____

_____

Reasons: _____

_____

_____

_____

_____

_____

Exercise 21.8

Both Singapore and Malaysia have laws that state that a person who perpetrates a crime with a gun (or deadly weapon), whether or not anyone is actually killed during the crime, will be executed. What do you think of this law?

_____

_____

_____

Do you think that capital punishment is a deterrent to criminals? _____

Do you believe in capital punishment? _____

Do you think that tougher penalties will reduce the number of gun-related deaths?

_____

Statistics indicate that places that have tough gun laws do have a lower number of deaths from guns. In 1990, there were only 87 handgun deaths in Japan, 22 in the United Kingdom, and 13 in Sweden. In the United States, on the other hand, there were over 10,500. On the lines provided, write your opinion about guns, gun control, and tougher penalties for gun-related crime.

_____

_____

_____

_____

_____

_____

Exercise 21.9

Work in pairs or groups. Discuss your answers concerning capital punishment and other tough penalties for gun-related crimes.

Language Review

Use the vocabulary to complete the sentences. Make grammatical changes when necessary.

fire	attach	exuberant	security
release	stark	by mistake	costume
inhabit	imitate	dress up as	take place
regulate	justify	cut down on	smuggle

1. Though many of the children at the Halloween Party were _____ ghosts

    and monsters, I think the most popular _____ at the party was a witch.

2. These birds _____ this area in the summer and migrate south during the winter.

3. Most banks have at least one _____ guard on duty during regular working hours.

4. The accident _____ at the intersection of Green and Wilcox.

5. She was _____ from prison after serving 7 years for armed robbery.

6. A thermostat _____ the temperature in a room.

7. In _____ contrast to the poor shacks near the river, there are huge homes just a few blocks away that obviously cost a fortune to build.

8. Without a paper clip, I can't _____ this report to the letter.

9. They brought the wrong books _____ and had to go back to get the right ones.

10. This is not real fur; it's _____.

11. The government has begun many new tough procedures, including more extensive border controls, in an attempt to _____ _____.

12. When the soldier _____ his gun, the kids immediately covered their ears.

Exercise 21.3: One in four American homes has a gun in it, so the number is 25 percent.

Unit 22

Don't Forget the TIP
(To Insure Promptness)

Mario's Italian Restaurant

1	Spaghetti	$9.50
1	Steak Dinner	14.80
2	Salads	6.00
1	Soft drink	1.50
1	tomato juice	2.20

Thanks!   8% tax   34.00
                     5.44
          TOTAL $ 39.44

What's a good amount for a tip?

Exercise 22.1

Tipping

In many places around the globe, tipping is an accepted custom, something that you are expected to do. In some countries, such as Japan, tipping is not done. Even in the United States, where tipping in restaurants, for example, is the norm, some people do not agree with this practice.

Tipping comes from the words "to insure promptness," which is the supposed purpose of tipping. Write your own opinion about tipping. Is tipping a good practice?

_____

_____

_____

Exercise 22.2

In small groups, discuss your answers to exercise 22.1.

Exercise 22.3

With a partner or in small groups, discuss the answers to these questions about tipping.
1. In a restaurant, how much of a tip do you usually leave?
2. Does tipping really "insure promptness" as it was intended to do?
3. Have you ever deliberately not left a tip? Describe the circumstances.
4. Why do we tip a waiter or waitress but not a flight attendant? (Both serve us food.)
5. Why do we tip the person who cuts our hair but not a doctor?
6. What kinds of professions do we usually tip?

Exercise 22.4

Read this case involving a tip at a restaurant.

> Maurice McParland, 31, was a waiter at a restaurant in London. One evening an incident involving a customer and the tip he left for McParland cost McParland his job.
>
> When the customer had finished dinner, McParland presented him with the bill for $42.75. The customer gave the waiter the amount of the bill, $42.75, plus a tip of $2.25. When McParland saw that the tip was so little (5 percent), he handed the tip back to the customer and remarked, "I think you need this more than me." The customer complained to the management, and for this action McParland was fired.
>
> McParland felt that he was fired unfairly. He said that the tip was "a bit of an insult." He claimed damages against the restaurant management of $1,800. The case went to an industrial tribunal, a special panel in Great Britain that hears employment grievances.

Exercise 22.5

If you were on the panel, would you make the restaurant pay? _____

Write two or three reasons for your decision._____

_____

_____

_____

Exercise 22.6

Work in small groups. Discuss your decision and your reasons. When you finish, read the tribunal's decision on page 176.

Language Review

Use the vocabulary to complete the sentences. Make grammatical changes when necessary.

globe	the norm	prompt	deliberately	circumstances
remark	grievance	dismiss	compensate	insult

1. Today's temperature got up to 72 degrees, but that's certainly not _____ for this area for this time of the year.

2. Trains in Japan almost always arrive and depart _____.

3. It would be a huge _____ to tell the host or hostess of a party that the food was not delicious.

4. The president's _____ that we might need higher taxes next year has

   drawn a great deal of interest as well as anger from the general public.

5. I'm sorry, but under these _____, I cannot continue to work for this company.

6. Does anyone know the record for the fastest time in which any kind of plane

   was able to go completely around the _____?

7. I don't think it was an accident. I think he _____ set the house on fire in order to collect the insurance money.

8. Before the professor _____ the class, he announced the title of the next essay that was due.

9. The workers were angry, so they made a list of all their _____ and gave this list to the boss for his consideration.

10. Because she was injured in the wreck and could not work for six months, she

    received a rather large sum of money as _____.

Unit 23

Drinking and Driving

If you drink, don't drive. If you drive, don't drink. It's simple.

Exercise 23.1

Discuss your answers in groups or as a class.
a. What does the illustration mean?
b. Have you heard this message before?
c. Have you ever had an alcoholic beverage and then driven a car? When?
d. Have you ever been a passenger in a car in which the driver had had a drink before he started driving? When? Were you worried or afraid?
e. Have you ever had an accident while driving under the influence of alcohol?

Exercise 23.2

Examine these statistics on the relationship between alcohol and motor vehicle accidents.

Statistics, 1994	
Deaths from motor vehicle accidents	43,000
Alcohol-related motor vehicle accidents	17,461 (44% of the first total)
Cost of alcohol-related motor vehicle accidents	$32.7 billion (1992)

Source: Data from National Safety Council, in *The World Almanac & Book of Facts 1996* (Mahwah, NJ : Funk & Wagnalls, 1995).

Exercise 23.3

a. What is your reaction to these statistics? Are you surprised or did you know this information already?

_____

_____

_____

_____

_____

b. Do people in your country drink and drive? What is the general attitude toward this? Is it accepted?

_____

_____

_____

_____

_____

c. What happens if someone is caught drinking while driving? What are the laws and penalties in your country?

_____

_____

_____

_____

_____

d. In Japan, although drinking with friends at restaurants and pubs at night is quite common, drinking and driving is not so common. The penalty for drunk driving is quite stiff. In addition, there is a special taxi arrangement for drunk drivers called "dai ko," which is composed of two symbols meaning "exchange" and "go." The drunk driver rides in the front passenger seat of his own car and one of two taxi drivers drives this car home according to the passenger's directions. The taxi follows. When the passenger reaches his home, the driver of his car returns as the passenger of the taxi that followed. The cost is not much more than just a regular taxi ride home. Would this system work in the United States or your country? Why or why not?

_____

_____

_____

_____

_____

Exercise 23.4

Work in groups. Discuss your perceptions and opinions about the topic of drinking and driving. Refer to the questions and your answers in exercise 23.3 if you need guidance.

Exercise 23.5

Read this passage about organizations that aim to cut down on the problem of drinking and driving, especially among young people.

> Alcohol is connected to about half of all motor vehicle deaths of 15- to 19-year-olds. In 1989, for example, 2,776 people in this age category who were killed in motor vehicle accidents had been drinking. In addition, 80,000 others were injured. Though these numbers are shocking enough, they used to be even higher before drinking and driving started to become socially unacceptable in the 1980s.
>
> To combat these terrible, frightening statistics, two national organizations have sprung up. One is called MADD, which stands for Mothers Against Drunk Driving. This organization, which was started by mothers who had lost children in motor vehicle accidents involving alcohol, works to make the public more aware of the dangers of drinking and driving and to strive for tougher laws and sentences for drunk drivers. Another organization is SADD, which stands for Students Against Driving Drunk. This group now has chapters in approximately 30,000 junior high schools, high schools,

and colleges, but the vast majority are in high schools. Young people and their parents sign a "Contract for Life" in which the young people agree to call home for transportation at any time if they or their friends have been drinking. In return, the parents pledge to pick up their children or pay for a taxi without asking any questions or giving the children any hassles. Perhaps because of the work of these organizations, the term "designated driver," a person in a group who is selected ahead of time as the driver and who will not have any alcohol during the evening out, has now become a part of normal English usage.

Exercise 23.6

In groups, discuss the work of MADD and SADD.

a. MADD works to stiffen the penalties for drunk driving. Do you support stiffer penalties? Why or why not?

b. What about the work of SADD? How would your parents react to the "Contract for Life"? (If you are an adult now, how would you react to this if your children wanted to sign it? Could you agree not to hassle them even if they were drunk when they called you?)

c. Are there any groups or movements similar to MADD or SADD in your country? If not, do you think there is a need? How would such a group go over in your country?

Exercise 23.7

Role-Play

Work in groups of three or four. Each student should do *one* of the roles (A, B, C, or D). When everyone has finished writing in step 1, do the role-play mentioned in step 2.

Role A: Imagine that you are at a party with two other friends. All three of you have been drinking. It is time to go home now. Since you are members of SADD, you want to call your parents, but your friend who is driving says he's OK. What do you think the three of you should do? Why?

Role B: Imagine that you are at a party with two other friends. All three of you have been drinking. It is time to go home now. Since you are members of

SADD, you want to call your parents, but you are the driver and are worried that your parents might get mad if you call them up at this hour of the night. What do you think the three of you should do? Why?

Role C: Imagine that you are at a party with two other friends. All three of you have been drinking. It is time to go home now. Since you are members of SADD, it is possible to call your parents, but your friend who is driving says he's OK. It is rather late and your parents are probably sleeping quite soundly. Your other friend who is not driving seems worried about the driver's condition and wants to call your parents. What do you think the three of you should do? Why?

Role D: Imagine that one of your children is at a party with two other friends. All three of them have been drinking. It is time to go home now. Since they are members of SADD, it is possible to call you, the parents. It is rather late and your are sleeping quite soundly. What do you think the three of them should do? Should they call you? Why or why not? If your child calls you up, what will you do? (Since you are the parent, it is possible that you might not get a chance to talk if the three teens decide not to call you. If this is the case, then you should do a role-play with your child when he reaches home. Confront him and ask him why he didn't call you as the Contract for Life calls for.)

Step 1. Write your thoughts as the person in your new role:

_____

_____

_____

_____

_____

_____

_____

_____

_____

_____

Step 2. Role-play in groups of three or four.

Language Review

Each question contains an italicized vocabulary item from this unit. Show that you understand the meaning of the italicized item by answering the question.

1. What kind of *vehicle* did you last drive? _____ What kind of *vehicle*

   did you first drive? _____ How old were you then? _____

2. What are some steps that the government can do to *combat* drugs in schools?

   _____

3. What does etc. *stand for?* _____ What does inc. *stand for?*

   _____ What does a red ribbon symbol *stand for?*

   _____

4. Have you ever been a *designated driver?* If yes, when was the last time? If no,

   why not? _____

   _____

5. What is one thing that is a *hassle* to do? _____

   _____

6. What is one thing that really makes you *mad?* _____

   _____

Unit 24

The Neighbors' Christmas Decorations

What would you do if 30,000 people came to your neighbor's house every December?

Exercise 24.1

Read this story about a family that decorates their house for Christmas much more than most people do.

Jennings and Mitzi Osborne live in a suburb of Little Rock, Arkansas. They began decorating their house for Christmas in 1986. As many families also do, each year the Osbornes have added more and more lights and decorations.

However, the situation at the Osbornes' home is different from other people's Christmas decorations. Their 1992 decorations included 1.6 million lights, and an estimated 30,000 people came to see the Osbornes' house.

It is the large number of people flocking to see the Osbornes' house that has the neighbors up in arms. They say they are tired of living next to a "Yuletide Disneyland." Olga Elwood, who lives two houses away, said, "It's a traumatic thing." The neighbors say that the traffic problems are horrendous. They are also tired of the crowds who walk across their yards and even picnic on their front lawns.

A local T.V. station conducted a poll and found that 90 percent of those polled are against the Osbornes' neighbors. However, the neighbors say that they have put up with this for years and only took the problem to court the year Mr. Osborne bought houses on both sides of his own, with the intention of tripling the Christmas display.

For comparison, you should know that the gigantic tree at Rockefeller Center in New York has 30,000 lights on it; the Osbornes' display has more than 50 times as many lights. In 1989, when the Osbornes turned on their lights, a transformer blew and darkened part of the neighborhood for a while. (They now have their own transformer.)

The neighbors had enough, and they took the Osbornes to court. They want their neighborhood peace back whether this means making the Osbornes take down or cut back on their Christmas display.

Exercise 24.2

If you were the judge, what would your decision be? Give at least two or three reasons for your answer.

Exercise 24.3

Work in pairs or small groups. Compare and discuss your answers to exercise 24.2. Try to agree on one answer (although your reasons may vary of course). When you have reached a group consensus, read page 176 to find out what the courts said.

Exercise 24.4

Role-Play

Work in small groups (four to six people). Each person should do *one* of these communication activities: 1, 7, 21, 30, 48, 54. (In each group, at least one person should do 1 and 7. It is possible for more than one person in the group to do 7.)

Step 1. Write who you are on this line: _____

Step 2. What are your feelings about what is happening? Why do you feel this way? Write your responses on these lines:

_____

_____

_____

_____

_____

Step 3. Now work in groups. You are the person in step 1. Introduce yourself. Tell your opinion of the problem. Tell the group what you think should happen and why. Feel free to ask the other members questions or to comment on their statements during the discussion.

Language Review

Match the definition from the right column with the correct word from the left column.

Vocabulary	Definition
____ 1. suburb	a. survey people's opinions about a topic
____ 2. flock	b. increase by three times

____ 3. up in arms   c. reduce or decrease

____ 4. traumatic   d. a residential community on the outskirts of a city

____ 5. conduct a poll   e. tolerate

____ 6. put up with   f. a large group of birds; to travel in a large group

____ 7. triple   g. disassemble; the opposite of *put up*

____ 8. lawn   h. extremely shocking

____ 9. take down   i. extremely angry about something

____ 10. cut back on   j. an area planted with grass

Unit 25

You Can Be the Judge: Who Is the Winner?

```
┌─────────────────────────────────────────────────────────────────┐
│ THE LOTTERY          THE LOTTERY           THE LOTTERY            │
│   IIII I II       I      I III I III I I IIII II                  │
│     MEGABUCKS  :                   :   :  21809                   │
│   A: 5-6-11-29-31-38 :              : 4 :  260                    │
│                   : SEP 17 94 : 5 : 02002                         │
│                   :$1.00 : 3 : 59757                              │
│   :IIII II  IIIIIIIII IIIIIIIII II I  II I  I I I  .III           │
│ MEGABUCKS        THE NUMBERS GAME          MASS·CASH              │
└─────────────────────────────────────────────────────────────────┘
```

You could win a million dollars!!!

Exercise 25.1

Read this court case about a lottery ticket.

In 1993, a young girl, who had gone to a grocery store with her mother, found two lottery tickets in the parking lot as she and her mother were coming out of the store. She picked up the tickets and took them home. That evening she learned that one of the tickets had a winning number on it. The prize for that ticket was $10,000.

Of course this story of a little girl finding such a lucky ticket made the news. When Dudley Havey heard the news, he was sure that it was *his* ticket. He had bought two tickets at about the time the girl was in the store with her mother. When he got home, he realized that he must have dropped the tickets somewhere. He didn't think much about the situation until he heard about the young girl's story.

The clerk at the store, Dave Johnson, says that he is pretty sure that the two tickets that the girl found are the same ones Havey purchased. Johnson

---

remembers that Mr. Havey was in the store around the same time the girl and her mother were in the store. In addition, Mr. Johnson was able to check his books to verify the ticket numbers and the approximate time of purchase.

The Massachusetts State Lottery Commission is responsible for the sale of six million lottery tickets a day. The odds of winning $10,000 are approximately 144,000 to 1. When asked about this case, the head of the commission said that the tickets belong to the person in possession of them.

Mr. Havey is taking this case to court. He believes that the tickets are his and that any money should be his as well. His lawyer is citing an 1836 Massachusetts law which says that anyone finding lost money or goods worth three dollars or more must report it to the police within two days. The girl and her mother did not do this.

Exercise 25.2

If you were the judge, would you make the girl return the money to Mr. Havey?

_____

Write two or three reasons for your decision. _____

_____

_____

_____

Exercise 25.3

Work in small groups. Discuss your decision and your reasons. When you finish, read page 176 for the judge's decision.

Exercise 25.4

Read these two sayings that are related to this unit. Can you figure out the meanings? Can you figure out how they are related to this unit? Do these sayings favor the young girl or Mr. Havey? If you need help, ask your teacher or an English speaker to explain these sayings to you.

1. Finders keepers, losers weepers.

   Who does it favor (the girl or Mr. Havey) ? _____

   What does it mean? _____

   _____

   _____

   _____

2. Possession is nine-tenths of the law.

   Who does it favor (the girl or Mr. Havey) ? _____

   What does it mean? _____

   _____

   _____

   _____

Language Review

Read the key word in the left column. Circle the letter of the word that is related to the key word.

1. pretty	a. extremely	b. barely	c. rather
2. verify	a. promise	b. check	c. oppose
3. as well	a. also	b. therefore	c. good
4. figure out	a. draw	b. solve	c. escape
5. favor	a. reject	b. announce	c. prefer
6. weep	a. cry	b. blame	c. glance
7. possess	a. struggle	b. own	c. demonstrate
8. purchase	a. buy	b. drop	c. cite

Unit 26

Animals and Humans

Does it matter if these species disappear from our planet?

Exercise 26.1

Which of these animals do you recognize? Which of these animals have you actually seen (in a zoo, perhaps)?

Species	*Natural Habitat*
leopard	Africa, Asia
golden parakeet	Brazil
giant panda	China
bobcat	Central Mexico
brown bear	Continental United States
cheetah	Africa to India
tiger	Asia
American alligator	Southeastern United States
bald eagle	United States, Canada
American crocodile	Florida (U.S.)

Asian elephant   South-central and Southeast Asia
gorilla   Central and West Africa
California condor   Oregon, California (U.S.)
black rhinoceros   Sub-Saharan Africa

Exercise 26.2

Do you think that animal extinction/conservation merits more attention? In other words, do you think that this is a serious problem? Explain your answer.

_____

_____

_____

_____

_____

_____

_____

What are some things that we can do to help avoid the extinction of endangered species?

_____

_____

_____

_____

_____

Exercise 26.3

Work in groups. Discuss your ideas about animal conservation. Refer to the questions and answers in exercise 26.2.

Exercise 26.4

Read these four causes of the extinction of animal species. Each of the four is followed by actual examples of a species that became extinct due to that situation. Which one do you think is the most important cause of extinction? Place a check mark (√) by your answer.

____ a. Overkill. In 1850, the passenger pigeon was the most common vertebrate in North America; in fact, this species made up 40 percent of all the birds in North America. The bird was slaughtered in large numbers and was extinct by 1914.

____ b. Introduced predators. Stephen Island wrens used to inhabit parts of the New Zealand mainland as well as nearby Stephen Island. Rats aboard boats from Polynesia entered the New Zealand mainland and killed off the Stephen Island wren there. On Stephen Island, the lighthouse keeper's cat killed off the small island population of wrens.

____ c. Introduced competitors. The introduction of competitors may cause extinction but most likely results in limiting the natural area which the species may inhabit freely and safely.

____ d. Habitat alteration. The clearing of Cebu Island in the Philippines led to the extinction of all 10 of its native bird species.

Exercise 26.5

Work in pairs or small groups to discuss your answers to exercise 26.4. Which of the four causes the most destruction to the animal and plant species on the planet? When you have finished discussing your choices and the reasons for your choices, you may look at page 126 to find out the answer.

Exercise 26.6

The Endangered Species Act, a special U.S. law designed to protect animal and plant species that are in danger of becoming extinct, was passed in 1973. Though the law does indeed serve its purpose of protecting plant and animal species, it has been a very controversial law because it costs a great deal of money to enforce and has resulted in the loss of jobs in certain cases.

The Endangered Species Act currently includes more than 1,300 species with 912 of those species found in the United States. Since the law took effect, 40 percent of the U.S. endangered species have stabilized or begun to improve in numbers while another 30 percent continue to decline but are declining more slowly. The bald eagle, the national symbol of the United States, numbered only 417 in 1963, but by 1993 that number had increased to 4,017; the bald eagle can now be found throughout the lower 48 states.

Critics of the law point to the high costs (a 1990 government study concluded that it would cost $4.9 billion dollars to rescue the species then on the list). In addition, jobs are a very sensitive issue. The most well-known case involves the spotted owl, which inhabits forests in the northwestern states. To protect the spotted owl, logging activities were halted or severely restricted. One estimate puts the number of lost jobs at 50,000 to 100,000 as many mills and even some small towns closed down.

The question boils down to this: What is one species worth? For some, it could be an undiscovered AIDS drug; for others, it could be a certain amount of money. Where do you stand?

Write your opinion of this issue. Limit your response to 50–125 words. Give at least two reasons to support your opinion.

_____

_____

_____

_____

The black-necked crane, which lives in China, numbers only about 5,500 in total. In 1941, there were only 21 whooping cranes in the United States. Due to protection efforts, there are now 270.

Exercise 26.7

Work in groups. Discuss the issue of protecting endangered species. How important are these plant and animal species to the world? What do you say to the people who have lost jobs because of these species? (If possible, read and then bring in to class a brief article on the Endangered Species Act or the story of any one of the animals on the endangered list. Summarize your article in three to five sentences. Be sure to tell whether the article is more pro-animal or pro-human jobs.)

Exercise 26.8

Animals are used every day to test the effects of products such as skin creams and colognes as well as various medicines which may be harmful to humans. Because some of the testing causes the animals pain and/or death, many people are against this use of animals. It is even possible to find products that are labeled, "Not tested on animals" so that consumers can have this option if they wish. How do you feel about this use of animals? Give two or three reasons to support your view.

_____

_____

_____

_____

_____

_____

Exercise 26.9

There is also debate about the use of animals in biomedical research. Is it moral? Is it necessary? Read this excerpt, which discusses using animals in biomedical research.

> Nedim Buyukmihci, a veterinarian and professor of ophthalmology, wants to stop all use of animals in biomedical research. For him, alleviating human death is not a good enough excuse to inflict death on animals. "Is it the fault of animals that we humans are suffering disease and death?" he asked. Concerning the history of medical discoveries and cures resulting

from animal research, he said it was an unproven myth. He added, "When you critically and honestly evaluate it, we do animal experimentation not because we think it right, but because we think we will derive benefits from it and because we have the power to do so." William Morton, a veterinarian and director of the primate center at the University of Washington in Seattle, explained how monkeys are bred in a special setting on a small island in Indonesia and then brought to the United States, where they are injected with the AIDS virus. Many of the monkeys have died, and death is likely to be the fate of all of them. Morton said, "The dream, of course, is that one day one will survive and make medical history." He said that stopping animal research "would be devastating to research and to humanity. There will be no cure, no vaccine or progress in the fight against AIDS without the use of animal research." Two-thirds of all Nobel Prizes for medicine resulted from discoveries involving animal research. Practically all vaccines, including polio, rubella, smallpox, measles, and mumps, would not be available today were it not for animal testing.

Exercise 26.10

Now write your opinion of the use of animals in biomedical research. Is it acceptable? Why or why not? Try to come up with at least three reasons to support your point of view.

_____

_____

_____

_____

_____

_____

Exercise 26.11

Now discuss your opinions on this topic. Use your opinions from exercise 26.6 and 26.8 to help you get started. Can your group reach a consensus on this topic?

Exercise 26.12

How do you feel about the use of animal products for humans? Some people do not like using leather (animal skin) for shoes, belts, and purses, or rabbit tails for good luck charms; many others do not approve of using furs to make coats and hats. It is not uncommon to see famous personalities such as Brigitte Bardot protesting against the manufacture, sale, and wearing of animal furs. Write your opinion on this topic.

_____

_____

_____

_____

Exercise 26.13

Now work in small groups to discuss your opinions about the use of animal furs.

Exercise 26.14

Imagine that you have a small garden that you take care of during your free time. Recently an animal has been roaming through your small garden and damaging your plants. You tried several times to keep the animal out, but in the end you had to set a trap. When you found the animal trying to escape from the trap, you hit it on the head with a stick, killing the animal.

Was it OK to kill the animal? For each animal, circle a number, with 1 being 100 percent acceptable and 5 being 100 percent unacceptable.

a.   1   2   3   4   5   The animal was a snake.

b.   1   2   3   4   5   The animal was a dog.

c.   1   2   3   4   5   The animal was a cat.

d.   1   2   3   4   5   The animal was a bird.

e.   1   2   3   4   5   The animal was a rat.

f.   1   2   3   4   5   The animal was a turtle.

Exercise 26.15

Read this court case about a gardener who tried to keep an animal out of his garden.

In July 1994, Frank Balun of Hillside, New Jersey, tried to solve a problem he was having with his small tomato patch. An animal was raiding his tomato patch, so he set a trap to catch the culprit. He was relieved to see a rat in his trap, thinking that the perpetrator had finally been caught. However, just as he was checking the trap, he saw that the rat's head was out of the trap and that the rat was trying to escape. Mr. Balun hit the rat on the head several times. "My friend told me if they get their head out, they can wiggle their whole body out," he said. He said he was worried that the rat would get out and possibly bite him, his six-year-old twin grandchildren who were visiting, or neighbors. Mr. Balun called the humane society to come get the rat's body, and that's when the trouble began.

The director of the Associated Humane Society in Newark issued two tickets to Mr. Balun. One ticket was for needlessly abusing the rat and another was for killing the rat in a cage designed for trapping squirrels. For these crimes, Mr. Balun could be sent to jail for six months and fined $1,250.

Was what I did really a crime?

Exercise 26.16

If you were the judge, would you put Mr. Balun in jail and fine him $1,250? _____

Write two or three reasons for your decision. _____

_____

_____

_____

Exercise 26.17

Work in small groups. Discuss your decision and your reasons. When you finish, read page 176 for the actual result of this court case.

Language Review

Use the vocabulary to complete the sentences. Make grammatical changes when necessary.

make up	slaughter	due to	take effect	stabilize
decline	halt	boil down to	inhabit	option
alleviate	inflict	evaluate	breed	fate
devastating	practically	roam	pace	raid
relieve	culprit	wiggle	perpetrator	humane

1. _____ everyone in the class passed the test. In fact, only one student

   failed.

2. If you want to change your flight, the only _____ available to you is to leave on the early morning flight instead.

3. Water _____ almost three-fourths of the earth's surface. However,

   environmentalists are concerned about the _____ at which water is becoming polluted and therefore unusable.

4. Millions of years ago dinosaurs _____ the face of this planet.

5. The director gave her a test to _____ her secretarial skills.

6. The soldier shouted, "_____ or I'll shoot!"

7. Mark Twain was born when Halley's Comet passed above the earth and he

   believed that it was his _____ to die the next time it came over the
   earth.

8. If you can _____ your toes, then they're not broken.

9. Jan was _____ to hear the news that her husband had arrived safely.

10. _____ the bad weather, all flights in and out of Detroit were can-
    celed.

11. Though there are many issues involved, the situation _____ this: Do
    we value species or jobs more?

12. Muslims and Jews eat meat that has been _____ in a special way ac-
    cording to certain religious rules.

13. The effects of the hurricane were _____: houses completely destroyed,

    cars flattened by trees, and furniture scattered everywhere in the yards and in
    the streets.

14. Though she was in critical condition, doctors were happy today when her

    condition began to _____. They now expect a full recover though it
    will take some time.

Exercise 26.4: The answer is d, habitat alteration. Human beings are de-
stroying natural habitats in order to make way for farms to raise crops on
and ranches to breed cattle on. The problem of habitat destruction is great-
est in the tropical forests. Though tropical forests make up only 7 percent
of the planet's surface area, they contain half of the earth's living species
(plants and animals). For example, a square mile of tropical forest in Indonesia contains approximately 10 times as many species as the same size
tract in the United States. More importantly, many of the tropical forest
species inhabit only that specific part of that tropical forest, so clearing that
particular area of land would result in the extinction of that species. For
example, New Caledonia, a relatively small island in the Pacific Ocean, contains 3,000 plant species, and 80 percent of these are not located anywhere
else on the earth; but Britain, which is many times larger, has only 1,400

plant species, and only 1% of these are located only in Britain. Tropical forests are being eliminated at an alarming rate, perhaps as much as 75,000 square miles per year. Clearly illustrating this dangerous pace, Ecuador has already lost 50 percent of its tropical forests while Madagascar has lost 90 percent. Sadly, Madagascar was home to 250,000 species before the loss of its tropical forests.

Unit 27

How Old Is Your Mother?
(Should There Be an Age Limit?)

Exercise 27.1

For homework, answer these questions. Write one or two sentences to explain your answer.

1. What is the ideal age for a woman to have her first child? _____

   _____

   _____

2. At what age should a woman stop trying to become pregnant? _____

   _____

   _____

3. What is the ideal age for a man to have his first child? _____

   _____

   _____

4. At what age should a man not father (produce) any more children? _____

   _____

   _____

5. How old is a person usually when he or she becomes a grandparent for the first

   time? _____

   _____

   _____

Exercise 27.2

Discuss your answers to the questions in exercise 27.1

Exercise 27.3

Read this story and then answer the questions that follow.

In 1993, a 59-year-old British businesswoman gave birth to twins. Since her body was no longer producing its own eggs, she used donated eggs that had been implanted into her uterus at a clinic in Italy. In June 1994, an Italian woman, age 62, gave birth to a healthy baby. She also had undergone a similar procedure at the same clinic in Rome.

The medical procedure involves finding a donor. This is often a friend or family member. The egg donor receives hormones to increase egg production. The mother-to-be receives different hormones to prepare her body for pregnancy. When the donor begins to ovulate (produce eggs), the doctor inserts a thin needle to extract eggs from her ovaries. Then the eggs are mixed with sperm in a culture dish to create embryos. The doctor then inserts three to five embryos into the mother's womb. It usually takes more than one try for the woman to become pregnant, and sometimes multiple births can result.

Many women have undergone this procedure successfully. The only "new" aspect is the fact that more and more often the women using this procedure are in their late 30s, 40s, 50s, and even, as in the case of the Italian woman, 60s. By using younger donors and screening the recipients for health problems, doctors report that this procedure is as safe for over-50 mothers as it is for women in their 40s.

1. What is one good thing about what you just read? _____

_____

2. What is one bad thing about what you just read? _____

_____

3. What is your opinion of the events described? _____

_____

_____

_____

_____

_____

_____

Exercise 27.4

Group Work

Discuss your answers to exercise 27.3. Do most people support or oppose the events described? Try to reach a group consensus.

Exercise 27.5

Now read this situation and then answer the questions that follow.

It is not difficult to find people who will say that it is not good for a woman in her 50s or 60s to have a child. These people give many reasons (e.g., the mother will probably be dead by the time the child is in college or the mother will be too old to take care of the child when he or she is growing up). However, what about the father? If a 50-year-old man fathers a child, people might joke or say something good about the man's ability to father a child even at age 50. Is this fair?

Situation 1: The wife is 52 and the husband is 40. Is it OK for the woman to undergo egg implantation to become pregnant?

Situation 2: The wife is 40 and the husband is 52. Is it OK for the woman to undergo egg implantation to become pregnant?

Write your reaction to the information on the lines below. Is situation 1 different from situation 2? Why or why not? _____

_____

_____

_____

_____

_____

_____

Exercise 27.6

Now work in groups to discuss your answers to the previous exercise.

Exercise 27.7

Role-Play

Work in threes or fours. Roles: One person is the doctor, one is the mother, and the other is the father. The fourth person can be a good friend who is worried about the woman's health and age. Situation: A childless couple goes to see their doctor because they want to have a child using egg implantation. The mother is 45 and the husband is 39. The doctor has done this procedure many times with other women, but the oldest to date was 32. He has misgivings about implanting eggs into a woman her age. Of course the couple tries to convince the doctor that they should be given the right to have a child if they want to.

Your role: _____

Your position on this issue: _____

_____

_____

_____

_____

Language Review

Each question contains an italicized vocabulary item from this unit. Show that you understand the meaning of the italicized item by answering the question.

1. How old was your mother when she *gave birth to* you? _____

2. Have you ever *donated* money to an organization? What was the organization? What is its purpose? _____

   _____

   _____

3. Can you name something that a doctor might *implant* in a human? _____

   _____

4. Have you ever *undergone* an operation? When was it? _____

   _____

5. Have you ever had a tooth *extracted?* If so, describe the situation to your class-mates. _____

   _____

   _____

Unit 28

Out of the Closet:
Gay and Lesbian Issues

Equal rights for all?

Exercise 28.1

Read the following situations and indicate your reaction by circling 1 if you agree strongly, 2 if you agree somewhat, 3 if you are not sure, 4 if you disagree somewhat, and 5 if you disagree strongly. Then write your opinion about these statements. Be sure to include one or two reasons to explain your opinion.

a.   1   2   3   4   5   Gays face a lot of discrimination from society.

_____

_____

_____

b.   1   2   3   4   5   I try to avoid gay people whenever possible.

_____

_____

_____

c.   1   2   3   4   5   It is OK for an employer to fire a worker if the employer finds out that the worker is gay.

_____

_____

_____

d.   1   2   3   4   5   Gays should be allowed to marry (form legal partnerships).

_____

_____

_____

e.   1   2   3   4   5   If one of my good friends came out to me, I'd still be friends with that person.

_____

_____

_____

f.   1   2   3   4   5   Gays have chosen to be gay.

_____

_____

_____

g.   1   2   3   4   5   Being gay is against God.

_____

_____

_____

h.   1   2   3   4   5   Gays have rights equal to heterosexuals.

_____

_____

_____

i.   1   2   3   4   5   If my brother or sister were gay, I'd try to have
                              nothing to do with him or her.

_____

_____

_____

j.   1   2   3   4   5   People should keep their sexual orientation
                              completely private.

_____

_____

_____

Exercise 28.2

Work in groups to discuss your answers to exercise 28.1.

For which three questions do your group members have the widest variation in

answers? ___, ___, ___ Which statement is the most controversial? ___ Why is it

controversial? _____

_____

_____

_____

_____

Exercise 28.3

In 1993, *U.S. News & World Report* conducted a poll of Americans to examine their attitudes toward gay and lesbian issues. Can you fill in the percentages? Use these numbers: 50, 65, 44, 73, 90, 53.

_____ percentage of Americans who say they personally know someone who is gay and this familiarity tends to make them think more favorably about gay rights

_____ percentage of Americans who say they want to ensure equal rights for gay people

_____ percentage of Americans who oppose extending current civil rights laws to cover gays

_____ percentage of American gays who voted for Clinton in the 1992 presidential election

_____ percentage of Americans who favor teaching about gay orientation in sex education classes in public schools

_____ percentage of Americans who oppose same-sex marriages

Exercise 28.4

Compare your numbers with a partner. Then check your answers on page 140. Would these percentages be the same or similar in your country? What would be different? Why do you think this is so?

Exercise 28.5

A common argument against homosexuality is based on religion. The following passage, written by an ESL teacher, deals with religion and homosexuality.*

THE BIBLE AND US
Martha Clark Cummings

Sometimes some people, especially my ESL students, use the Bible as a rationale for their homophobia. "The Bible says it's forbidden," they say. In answer to this argument, I often reply that if we were going to adhere strictly to Biblical teachings, we would also have to consider the items listed below. The Bible says that:

— wives must be submissive to their husbands (I Peter 3:1)
— women are forbidden to teach men (I Timothy 2:12)
— women are forbidden to wear gold or pearls (I Timothy 2:9)

GLESOL Newsletter, January 1994. Reprinted by permission.

> — women are forbidden to wear clothing that "pertains to a man" (Deuteronomy 22:5)
> — shaving is forbidden (Leviticus 19:27)
> — wearing clothing of more than one fabric is forbidden (Leviticus 19:19)
> — the penalty for adultery is death by stoning (Deuteronomy 22:22)
>
> Finally, it helps to remind people of the little-remembered statement in Luke 12:57. Jesus said, "Why do you not judge for yourselves what is right?"

Now write your reaction on these lines. _____

_____

_____

_____

Exercise 28.6

Work in groups. Discuss the information in the previous exercise as well as your reaction to this information. Discuss various religious arguments against homosexuality.

Exercise 28.7

Do you think gays should be allowed to serve in the military? _____

Give two or three reasons to explain your answer. _____

_____

_____

_____

_____

Now take the opposing view. What do you think are two or three reasons to support that view? _____

_____

_____

_____

_____

Can gays serve in the military in your country? _____

Exercise 28.8

In groups, discuss your answers to exercise 28.7. What is the overall consensus of your group about this question?

Exercise 28.9

Read this case involving a military person who was kicked out of the military because he revealed that he is gay.

In May 1994, Petty Officer 1st Class Keith Meinhold appeared on a nationally broadcast television program to discuss gays in the military. At this time, the issue of allowing gays to serve openly in the military was a very heated topic in the United States. In the television program, Officer Meinhold stated publicly that he was a homosexual. In August, Officer Meinhold, who had served in the navy for 12 years with a good record, was dismissed from the navy with an honorable discharge according to the policy barring gay men and lesbians from military service. Meinhold disagreed with this decision on the grounds that his sexual orientation was not connected in any way with his military duties or his good military record.

Exercise 28.10

If you were the judge, what would you decide? Should Meinhold be kicked out of

the military? _____ Why do you believe this? _____

_____

_____

_____

_____

Exercise 28.11

Discuss your answers to the Meinhold case in small groups or with a partner. Do
you think that Meinhold should be kept out of military service? Should gay men
and lesbians be barred from serving in the military? When you have finished your
discussion, turn to page 176 to see what the judge actually decided.

Exercise 28.12

In some states, gays and lesbians cannot get teaching jobs. Do you think gays and

lesbians should be allowed to be teachers? _____ Why or why not? Give

two or three reasons to explain your answer. _____

_____

_____

_____

_____

Now take the opposing view. What do you think are two or three reasons to sup-

port that view? _____

_____

_____

_____

_____

_____

Exercise 28.13

In groups, discuss your answers to exercise 28.12. What is the overall consensus of your group about this question?

Exercise 28.14

A 1994 movie entitled *Philadelphia* presented the story of a promising lawyer who was fired because he had AIDS. If you have not seen this movie, watch it. Discuss the story in class.

Language Review

Use the vocabulary to complete the sentences. Make grammatical changes when necessary.

discrimination	partner	come out	have nothing to do with
controversial	ensure	oppose	phobia
adhere to	submissive	forbid	pertain to
adultery	heated	in any way	kick out (of)

1. The company president _____ the idea of forming a close _____

   with Simmons Corporation because of the numerous drawbacks for our company.

2. Jack was _____ the club for repeatedly not paying his dues on time.

3. Sarah has been trying to make up with her boyfriend, but he will

   _____ her.

4. Due to the fear of _____, it is difficult and sometimes impossible for

   gays and lesbians to _____ to their families, friends, and coworkers.

5. One hundred years ago, wives were expected to be _____ to their husbands, but this situation has changed for the most part.

6. Swimmers who cannot _____ the rules posted near the pool are not welcome to swim in this pool any more.

7. Abortion is certainly a very _____ topic in the United States. (two answers possible)

8. The judge granted the divorce on the grounds of _____.

9. Many people have a _____ of flying.

10. My question is not about the date of this bill; it _____ the amount of the bill.

> Exercise 28.3: The answers (in order) are: 53, 65, 50, 90, 44, 73.

Unit 29

Group Speaking Puzzle: Food, Endangered Species, and Colors

Exercise 29.1

Work in groups of three. Student A should look at communication activity 27, student B 33, and student C 42.

Step 1: Use the clues in your communication activities to solve the puzzle.

Step 2: When you have used all your clues, ask your partners for clues about the answers you do not know. In this step, students may use the clues in the communication activity, but you may not refer to the communication activity. Try to make up your own descriptions for the words whenever possible.

Exercise 29.2

Work in small groups. Discuss your answers to the following questions.

a. 7 down is a large city in England. Have you ever been there? Why is it a popular tourist destination? What are the most famous tourist sights?

b. 6 across is a kind of bird. Have you noticed this bird on American money? This bird was an endangered species but has recently been taken off the endangered list. Can you think of any animals that are on the endangered list? What about animals that have vanished?

c. 14 across is high in cholesterol, so many people limit their quantity of this kind of food. How many of these do most people in your class eat in a week? (Write your estimate here: _____.) To find out the answer, ask the other students in your class. How many do you eat in a week? In recent years, has this number increased, decreased, or remained the same? Why?

d. Have you ever seen 20 down? Do you believe that they really exist?

e. Have you ever played 24 across? Are you a good player? Explain the game to those students who are not familiar with it. What are some good strategies needed to win this game?

f. 13 across was the main theme covered in the movie *Philadelphia*. Did you see this movie? What is your opinion of the movie? What is the actor's name? Have you seen any of his other movies? (He won an Oscar for best actor for his role in this movie.)

g. 5 down is a color. What percentage of the students in your class will say this is their favorite color? (Write your estimate here: _____.) To find out the answer, ask the students in your class.

Language Review

Use the vocabulary to complete the sentences. Make grammatical changes when necessary.

strategy	vanish	fatal	dominate	sum
ingredient	yolk	alien	quantity	role

1. The _____ of an egg is one of the most important _____ for

making custard.

2. If you really want to save money, a good _____ is to buy a large

_____ of meat or vegetables, because larger packs are often cheaper

than smaller packs if you compare price per pound.

3. Our high school basketball team was so good that it completely _____
    all the other teams in our league.

4. The police now suspect that alcohol played a _____ in the

    _____ two-car accident that took place yesterday on Highway 63.

5. David Copperfield, a famous magician, made the Statue of Liberty _____
    in one of his best-known tricks.

Unit 30

The Bus Driver's Dilemma

What would you do if you found a case filled with cash?

Exercise 30.1

Read this strange but true story that happened on a bus.

> Sonja Kelly is a bus driver in San Francisco. Her job has few surprises and she follows more or less the same routine every working day.
>
> Recently Sonja found an envelope that a passenger left on her bus. At one of her stops, she walked to the seat where the envelope was lying, picked it up, and brought it back to her seat. Because of her tight schedule, she didn't bother to open it until later that day. When she did open it, she was shocked to find a stack of $100 bills. She began counting, "One, two, three, four" There were 146 bills for a grand total of $14,600.
>
> Sonja turned the money in to the lost and found office. There was no name or address on the envelope, but the passenger who had left the envelope on the bus eventually called the office looking for his envelope.

Exercise 30.2

No one but Sonja knew that she had found the envelope on her bus and no one but Sonja (and the passenger of course) knew the contents of the envelope until she turned it in to the lost and found office. How many of the students in your class would have done what Sonja did? Write your guess here now: _____. (Do not discuss this with a classmate yet.) If you had been Sonja, what would you have done? Why? _____

_____

_____

_____

Exercise 30.3

Work in small groups. Discuss your answers to exercise 30.2. What is your group's consensus on what you would do if you were Sonja? How accurate was your prediction of the number of students in your class who would have done what Sonja did?

Exercise 30.4

Imagine you are the owner of the envelope and you know that Sonja is the person who found the envelope and did the honest thing by turning it in to the lost and found office instead of keeping the money for herself. Would you give her a reward

of some kind? _____ If so, what would you give her? If you are thinking

of a monetary reward, what is a reasonable amount for a reward in this case?

_____

_____

Exercise 30.5

a. Discuss your answers to exercise 30.4. Try to reach a group consensus.
b. Turn to page 147 to find out what the real owner of the envelope actually did in this situation.
c. What is your reaction to what the owner did? How does this compare to your own answer in exercise 30.4 and to your group's consensus?

Exercise 30.6

Work with a partner(s) to write a dialogue for one of the following situations.
a. You go to a lost and found counter to find something you have lost. You finally find the item.
b. You find a stray cat, learn who the owner is through an announcement in the lost and found column in the newspaper, and call up the owner to arrange the return of the cat. The owner offers you a reward.

c. You have found a beautiful watch on the ground at the bus stop. You discuss with a friend what you should do with the watch.

Exercise 30.7

Role-Play

Take turns acting out your dialogues. Afterward, one student (from the audience) should make a brief oral summary of the dialogue (telling the characters, the general situation, and the conclusion).

Language Review

Use the vocabulary to complete the sentences. Make grammatical changes when necessary.

routine   stack   turn in   reward   counter   stray

1. A: What's the daily _____ at your job like?

   B: I work at the front _____ all day. Then at four o'clock, I do paperwork.

2. A: What are you going to do with that _____ of books by the door?

   B: Those are books I have to _____ to the library. They're due back today.

3. A: What a beautiful cat! How much did you pay for him?

   B: This cat? You must be joking. He's just a _____ that I started feeding.

4. A: Did you hear that the bank was robbed this morning?

   B: Yes, I did. The police are offering a _____ for information about the crooks.

Exercise 30.5: The envelope contained one hundred forty-six (146) $100 bills or $14,600. As a reward for finding and turning in the envelope of money, the owner gave Sonja $100.

Unit 31

You Can Be the Judge: May I Die?

Exercise 31.1

Read this court case about a medical and human dilemma.

Dr. Jack Kevorkian gained fame, or notoriety, depending on your opinion, for helping the terminally ill to end their lives. Dr. Kevorkian, who practices medicine in the state of Michigan, attends "medicides," a term Kevorkian uses for doctor- assisted suicides. In these medicides, which he has been attending since 1990, Dr. Kevorkian provided patients with the means to commit suicide.

On October 22, 1993, Dr. Kevorkian set up an apparatus that allowed Merian Frederick, a 72-year-old woman suffering from a debilitating nerve disease, to inhale carbon monoxide. About a month later, Dr. Kevorkian helped another doctor, Ali Khalili, die by a similar method.

Dr. Kevorkian helped a 30-year-old man with a degenerative nerve disease which had left the man paralyzed and in extreme pain. The doctor put a mask over the patient's face and connected it to a container of carbon monoxide. The patient then turned a knob to start the flow of the poisonous gas to himself. The man made a videotape a month before the actual medicide. The tape shows the man with one arm dangling, completely useless, while the man had difficulty moving his other arm. He was a l m o s t unable to swallow and took several minutes to get out these words: "I want to end it. I want to die."

Many of the patients that Dr. Kevorkian has assisted with medicides are terminally ill. Many are in extreme pain. For example, Dr. Khalili had cancer that had progressed to the point that his bones were fracturing and he had to use a morphine pump to control his pain. These patients chose to die rather than live.

In early 1992, the state of Michigan passed a law forbidding assisted suicides. This law was aimed specifically at Dr. Kevorkian. Dr. Kevorkian has challenged the law, saying that it is an invasion of a person's privacy, that a person has the right to die however and whenever he or she sees fit.

Under the current law, Dr. Kevorkian could be convicted of murder. The court must decide whether the law as it is written now is correct.

Exercise 31.2

If you were on the jury, what would you say? Is Dr. Kevorkian guilty of murder?

_____

Write two or three reasons for your decision. _____

_____

_____

_____

_____

Exercise 31.3

Step 1. For further information to consider, read this.

Opponents of medicides would like you to consider the following information.

It is true that Thomas Hyde deliberately tried to find Dr. Kevorkian in order to end his own life. Hyde hated the disease that had weakened his arms to the point that he couldn't even lift his own daughter. The illness had happened very quickly; within a year, Hyde could no longer walk or speak clearly, and he knew he was going to die.

However, the choice of suicide for such terminally ill people is much rarer than most people know. In a survey of 86 others with the same disease as Hyde, only 2 said they were sorry they were alive or dependent on a respirator. Medicide opponents say that we have underestimated the will or desire of people to live and should not use Hyde's decision to say that suicides with help from doctors are OK.

Step 2. Work in small groups. Discuss your decision and your reasons.

Step 3. When you finish your discussion, read the result of this case on page 177.

Exercise 31.4

What is your opinion about euthanasia? Write your thoughts here. _____

_____

_____

_____

_____

_____

Exercise 31.5

Work in small groups. Discuss your answers and reasons from exercise 31.4.

Exercise 31.6

Write your reactions to the following statements.

1. Life is a gift from God and we are not free to end it at our will.

_____

_____

_____

_____

2. If assisted suicides are legal, then we will have the problem of people showing up at doctors' offices wanting to die for a variety of different reasons. In other words, doctors (or some professional) will provide suicide on demand.

_____

_____

_____

3. Doctors are supposed to help people get better, not kill them.

_____

_____

_____

_____

4. Kevorkian considers the donation of organs one of the positive aspects of medicides.

_____

_____

_____

_____

Exercise 31.7

Work in small groups. Discuss your answers and reasons from exercise 31.6.

Exercise 31.8

Read this story of a terminally ill patient who chose not to commit suicide.

> Consider the case of Donna White. When she got sick, her pain was so bad she wished for anything to help her—pills, poison, starvation, Kevorkian. Her three biggest fears are the same three shared by many who are terminally ill: dying in pain, dying alone, and causing great financial or emotional distress to one's family. Instead of ending her own life, White found help through hospice care. The hospice nurse and her doctor worked together to get a better combination of medicines to get the pain under control. Because hospice care is about $80 a day (instead of $1,000 in a hospital), there was no great financial burden on her family. White also had a social worker who talked to her about death and who helped White to talk about her own death. White's case is not unusual; each year about 250,000 Americans who are terminally ill discover hospice care.

Exercise 31.9

Write your reaction here. Have you changed your opinion about medicide?

_____

_____

_____

_____

_____

Exercise 31.10

Read this true story of a young man with a severe medical problem.

> Benito "Benny" Agrelo is 15 years old. He has already undergone two liver transplants. Benny drew national attention because he refused to continue taking the painful anti-rejection drugs that he needs to keep his body's natural defense system from rejecting his new liver. Benny says that the medicine causes severe headaches and pain in his joints and makes him very irritable.
>
> When the Florida State social service agency found out that he was not taking his prescribed medicine, they forcibly hospitalized Benny and gave him the medicine.
>
> Benny has appealed to the courts to help him. Benny knows that not taking the medicine will probably cause him to die, but he says he would rather die in peace than continue to live in pain.

Exercise 31.11

If you were the judge, would you make Benny take the medicine that is needed to

keep him alive? _____ Write two or three reasons for your decision.

_____

_____

_____

_____

_____

Exercise 31.12

Work in small groups. Discuss your decision and your reasons. When you finish, read the outcome of this story on page 177.

Former President Richard Nixon and former First Lady Jacqueline Kennedy Onassis both made living wills.

Exercise 31.13

Read this brief passage on living wills.

> Before they died in 1994, two famous Americans, former President Richard M. Nixon and former first lady Jacqueline Kennedy Onassis, performed one last public service: they helped focus attention on living wills. A living will is a set of instructions in which people record in writing their wishes about medical treatment in case they become unable to communicate during their final days. For example, a person might not want to be put on a life support system which he or she feels would only prolong life without hope of true recovery. A person's right to accept or refuse treatment is protected under the Constitution. An estimated 50 million Americans have living wills.

Exercise 31.14

Have you ever heard of living wills? (If not, ask a native speaker or find some information in English about this topic.) Do you think that living wills are a good idea? Why or why not?

_____

_____

_____

_____

_____

Exercise 31.15

Work in small groups. Discuss your decision and your reasons. What is your group's consensus? Does anyone in the group have a personal experience with a living will or a situation in which a living will would have been helpful?

Language Review

Part A. Use the vocabulary to complete the sentences. Make grammatical changes if needed.

reject	joint	irritate	consequence	pass away
former	perform	will	prolong	in case

1. _____ President Richard Nixon _____ in 1994. His wife

   had died the previous year.

2. Elbows and knees are called hinge _____.

3. A document telling to whom a deceased person's possessions will go is a

   _____.

4. One of the _____ of World War II was a divided Germany.

5. _____ you have any questions about this paper, call me tonight.

6. She _____ their offer because the job did not include insurance

   and health benefits.

7. Modern medicine can sometimes _____ a life but at great cost.

8. Before I've had my morning cup of coffee, I'm very _____.

Part B. Read the key word in the left column. Circle the letter of the word related to the key word.

1.	notorious	a.	difficult	b. known	c. further
2.	terminal	a.	end	b. guilty	c. contract
3.	set up	a.	consider	b. change	c. assemble
4.	flow	a.	movement	b. wish	c. provide
5.	suicide	a.	water	b. death	c. beside
6.	invasion	a.	help	b. report	c. entry
7.	underestimate	a.	below	b. summarize	c. clarify
8.	obligation	a.	mannerism	b. duty	c. machine
9.	show up	a.	appear	b. practice	c. demonstrate
10.	on demand	a.	on purpose	b. that pays	c. when requested
11.	starvation	a.	apparatus	b. dangling	c. food
12.	distress	a.	relaxation	b. anxiety	c. probability

Unit 32

Check Your Emergency IQ

Exercise 32.1

Test Yourself

Read these six situations involving emergency first aid and choose what you consider to be the best answer. Write one or two sentences to explain why you chose your answer (and not the other answer choices).*

1. Your three-year-old son has just swallowed lighter fluid. You should immediately
    a. call the poison control center.
    b. feed him syrup of ipecac.
    c. take him to the emergency room.

    Reason: _____

    _____

    _____

2. You're visiting your father-in-law when he suddenly slumps to the floor, unconscious and without a pulse. What's your first move?
    a. Dial 911.
    b. Begin cardiopulmonary resuscitation (CPR), including mouth to-mouth and chest-pumping.

*Quiz researched by Valerie Fahey. Reprinted from *Health,* ©1994.

Reason: _____

_____

_____

3. You spill boiling water and badly burn your arm. You should
   a. wrap ice cubes in cloth and hold them on the burn for ten minutes.
   b. run cold water on the burn for 10 minutes.
   c. rub chilled butter into the burn.

Reason: _____

_____

_____

4. You've just pulled your five-year-old niece unconscious from the swimming pool. She doesn't have a pulse. You should
   a. begin CPR immediately.
   b. run to dial 911, then attempt CPR.

Reason: _____

_____

_____

5. Your husband badly sprains his ankle playing basketball in the backyard. You should help him to
   a. soak his ankle in hot water.
   b. lie down with his ankle propped up and wrapped in ice.
   c. walk gingerly around to keep the blood circulating.

Reason: _____

_____

_____

6. A friend who's diabetic is wandering around at a picnic acting drunk, yet has had only one beer. You should

a. speed him to the hospital before he lapses into diabetic coma.
b. get him to take his insulin.
c. feed him juice or a soft drink.

Reason: _____

_____

_____

Exercise 32.2

Work in threes. Take turns saying what your answer for each question is and why you believe your answer is correct. When you have discussed your answers for all six situations, read the correct answers on page 160. Which answers are the most surprising to you? Why?

Exercise 32.3

Describe a real emergency situation that you experienced, saw personally, heard about, or saw on TV or in a movie *or* you can make up a story about an imagined emergency situation. Do *not* tell anyone whether your story is real or imagined.

Write out your story for homework. Use a dictionary to get vocabulary that you do not know. At the next class meeting, students will take turns telling their emergency story and the other students will have to ask questions to better understand what really happened. Then the listeners will have to vote whether the story is real or imagined. Good luck!

_____

_____

_____

_____

_____

_____

_____

_____

Language Review

Match the definition from the right column with the correct word from the left column.

	Vocabulary	*Definition*
___	1. syrup	a. support (in a vertical position)
___	2. slump	b. not function properly
___	3. pulse	c. put in water for a long time
___	4. chill	d. most important item
___	5. conscious	e. expand, enlarge
___	6. soak	f. become cool
___	7. prop up	g. cure, treatment
___	8. circulate	h. logical, orderly
___	9. go haywire	i. droop or fall
___	10. top priority	j. (chemical) substance that causes injury or death
___	11. poison	k. move or flow
___	12. coherent	l. heartbeat
___	13. swell	m. thick, sweet, sticky liquid
___	14. remedy	n. awake, aware

Exercise 32.2:

1. a. Definitely have syrup of ipecac on hand in case you need to induce vomiting, but don't use any poison remedy without first checking with the poison control center. In this case, vomiting could force the gas into the boy's lungs or injure his esophagus. The poison center will ask the boy's symptoms and help you decide whether to get him to a hospital or just let the fluid pass naturally through his digestive tract.

2. a. Because cardiac arrest in adults is usually caused by ventricular fibrillation, in which the heart's electrical signals go haywire, CPR is rarely effective. It saves lives only 1 in 10 times. Starting CPR after the 911 call is recommended, but the top priority is to get the defibrillator machine carried by most emergency teams to your father-in-law's side.

3. b. Though butter and ice were once recommended for burns, they're now no-nos. Ice can further damage the skin, while butter is just ineffective. After running water on a burn, seek medical attention for blistered, charred, or peeling burns.

4. a. Usually a child's heart stops because he or she isn't getting air, so the top priority here is CPR. Give one mouth-to-mouth breath and pump her chest every three seconds for at least one minute before carrying her to the phone to dial 911. Then try CPR again.

5. b. Do everything contained in the acronym RICE—rest, ice, compression (with an Ace bandage), and elevation. If swelling hasn't gone down at all in 48 hours, call a doctor; the injury could require a cast.

6. c. Low blood sugar due to too much insulin or not enough food can cause incoherence in a diabetic. With the sugar in four ounces of juice or soft drink or, alternatively, a candy bar, he should be back to normal in 15 minutes. If he's still shaky, a bit more sugar might be needed.

Communication Activities

Communication Activity 1

Imagine that you are Mr. Osborne. Write your name on the line in step 1 on page 112. Then follow the instructions there.

Communication Activity 2

You are opposed to gun control. Your main reason for opposing it is that although the average person will not be able to get a gun, criminals will continue to get guns illegally. This will mean that instead of the current situation in which some of the good people have guns and some of the bad people have guns, only the bad people will have guns.

Communication Activity 3

Write this line on page 76: He wasn't very hungry, so he just asked for a hamburger and a cup of coffee.

Communication Activity 4

Write this line on page 37: As we neared the ground, I heard the loud rumble of the landing gear going down.

Communication Activity 5

1. *Don't put off until tomorrow what you can do today*. This proverb means that the best time to do something is usually right now. We should not wait until later (tomorrow) to do what we can do right now because we might not be able to do the same thing in the future. For example, you have to wash your car and the weather is good today. You feel a little tired, but the weather might be cold tomorrow. Your friend tells you, "Don't put off until tomorrow what you can do today."

2. *Too many cooks spoil the broth*. Broth means a kind of simple soup. If two cooks are in the kitchen at the same time trying to cook the same food, problems will happen. Only one person should be in charge of a project. For example, two people are planning a party. Person A makes the food but doesn't get any music because he thinks B is going to get the music. However, B makes the food but doesn't get any music because he thinks A is going to take care of

the music. The end result is a party with food but no music—and no drinks—because they both thought the other was in charge of that. "Too many cooks spoil the broth."

Communication Activity 6

Write this line on page 66: A man went to see his doctor because he was over-weight.

Communication Activity 7

Imagine that you are one of the Osbornes' neighbors. Write your name on the line in step 1 on page 112. Then follow the instructions there.

Communication Activity 8

Write this line on page 76: One of the motorcyclists said to the waitress, "He isn't such a tough guy. He didn't even say anything."

Communication Activity 9

1. *Where there's a will, there's a way.* This proverb means that if a person has the will (strong desire or determination) to do something, then surely there is a way to accomplish that goal. For example, while planning for a dinner party, A asks B "Do you think we can put together this dinner for under $50?" B, who thinks that this can be done even though it will be difficult, replies, "Where's there a will, there's a way."
2. *The early bird gets the worm.* The message behind this proverb is that doing things early is very important. The worm represents your goal and the bird represents you. If you don't get to a place (or situation) early, then perhaps another bird (person) will get the goal first. For example, if there is a job adver-tised at an office, you should check it out as soon as you can because if you don't hurry, someone else might beat you there and get the job instead of you: "The early bird gets the worm."

Communication Activity 10

You support gun control. Your main reason for supporting it is that having more guns on the streets won't solve the problem. In fact, more guns on the street will make the situation worse. We need gun control to help reduce the number of guns out there.

Communication Activity 11

Write this line on page 37: Since I fly quite frequently, I was not worried by the three tries to land; however, I noticed that the man next to me was extremely nervous.

Communication Activity 12

Write this line on page 66: The patient asked, "So how many do I take every day?"

Communication Activity 13

Here are some of the puzzle clues. Do not show this to the other students in your group. You may read and discuss the clues.

1 down:	Pluto is one of these	3 down: Wimbledon is a site for this sport
4 down:	He wanted to phone home	
7 down:	word before orange or apple	6 across: "the" in Spanish or French
10 down:	a monster	9 across: peanut butter — jelly
13 across:	a famous movie, *Out of —*	15 across: to the east of Europe
16 across:	a country in Europe	18 across: a kind of green vegetable
12 down:	You move these when you chew your food.	21 across: negative
17 down:	the letter after *C* and the letter before *L*	
20 down:	a verb used with homework	

Communication Activity 14

1. *A bird in the hand is worth two in the bush*. Imagine a hunter who already has one bird in his hand. He then sees two birds in a nearby bush. If he goes after the two in the bush, he might not get them and the bird he has in his hand now might get away. This proverb means it is better to be satisfied with a sure thing (the bird in the hand) than to strive for something that looks desirable but might not happen (the two birds in the bush), because going after the unknown might cause you to lose what you already have.
2. *When life gives you lemons, make lemonade*. Lemons are sour things; they represent things that are not pleasant. Lemonade represents something good that you can make from something that is bad (the sour lemons). This proverb means that when something bad happens to you, try to do something good with the bad thing. Try to make the best of a bad situation instead of just complaining about it.

Communication Activity 15

Write this line on page 76: Just as the truck driver was about to bite into his burger, two guys pulled into the parking lot on really big motorcycles and raced their engines.

Communication Activity 16

It is true that what Captain Haynes was able to do with flight 232 was indeed remarkable. Perhaps a less experienced captain would not have been as successful with the same situation. However, there are many other captains who have reached the age of 60 who are beginning to lose the sharpness of certain important senses, such as sight or hearing, or stamina. Yes, it is true that there are many older people who do not fall into this category, but how will we judge them and are we willing to take a chance with the safety of so many passengers? And what will the age limit be if not 60? Is 65 better? Then what about 66 or 67?

Communication Activity 17

Write this line on page 37:   Last week I flew from Los Angeles to New York, a long flight that lasted for about six hours.

Communication Activity 18

Write this line on page 66: The doctor listened and then gave the man a bottle of pills.

Communication Activity 19

1. *The grass is always greener on the other side of the fence*. We are never content with what we have. When we look at what our neighbor has, it always looks better than what we have. The fence represents the fence between our own house and our neighbor's house, and grass represents anything. A and B are talking about their jobs. A says, "I hate my job. I wish I could work at that new company down the street." B replies, "I know the grass always looks greener on the other side of the fence, but don't be silly. You have a good job with a good salary and good benefits. Anyway, I heard that that new company is having financial problems and might have to close down soon, so stay where you are!"
2. *Don't put all your eggs in one basket*. This proverb means that it's not a good idea to count on only one thing to provide you with money or other necessities. If a person plans to put all his money into a new company, his banker might offer this advice: "I know the company sounds good, but it could be dangerous for you. Don't put all your eggs in one basket."

Communication Activity 20

You are opposed to gun control. Your main reason for opposing it is that it can't be enforced properly. Yes, gun control may work in a small country with borders that are easily checked, but the United States is a big country with a tremendously long coastline. Even if we had extremely strict gun control laws, it would be relatively easy to smuggle guns into the United States.

Communication Activity 21

Imagine that you are a police officer who directs the increased Christmas traffic in the neighborhood. Write your name on the line in step 1 on page 112. Then follow the instructions there.

Communication Activity 22

Write this line on page 76: One day a truck driver stopped at a small roadside café for a bite to eat.

Communication Activity 23

Write this line on page 37: The man turned to me and said, "You don't get it. I am a pilot and I *do* know what they are doing!"

Communication Activity 24

Write this line on page 66: The doctor then added, "Drop them on the floor and pick them up. Do this three times a day."

Communication Activity 25

1. *When in Rome, do as the Romans do.* This proverb means that you should adopt the customs or habits of the people wherever you are. If you go to Japan, you should learn to take your shoes off at the front door. If you go to Saudi Arabia, you should learn to eat with your right hand instead of with kitchen utensils. If you begin working at a company where all the men wear light blue shirts with crazy ties, you should do the same, because "when in Rome, do as the Romans do."

2. *Don't count your chickens until they've hatched.* If a farmer has a chicken that laid 10 eggs, the farmer might start calculating how much he'll make by selling 10 fat hens. However, this is premature. There are many things that might

happen to change the farmer's expected result. Some of the eggs might get cracked or some of the eggs might not hatch. This proverb means that you should not assume something until it actually happens.

Communication Activity 26

You are a big supporter of gun control. Gun control has indeed worked in many other countries. In Japan, people are prohibited from owning any kind of weapon and the death rate from guns in Japan is incredibly low. In Malaysia and Singapore, where using a gun in any kind of crime carries the death penalty even if no one is killed, incidents with guns are very rare.

Communication Activity 27

Here are some of the puzzle clues. Do not show this to the other students in your group. You may read and discuss the clues.

21 across: less than two
9 down: first word in many yes/no questions
15 down: what the green light means
13 across: a fatal disease
19 down: the total in addition
4 down: exercise class in school
1 down: important ingredient on a cheeseburger

10 across: used to show possession sometimes
22 across: a dish in the sky
16 down: like a small river
14 across: the yolk and the white are its two parts
24 across: Park Place and Boardwalk are in this game

Communication Activity 28

Write this line on page 37: We flew out past the airport and came back for a second attempt.

Communication Activity 29

Write this line on page 76: The truck driver surprised everyone by not saying anything. He just got up, paid his bill at the register, and went to his truck.

Communication Activity 30

Imagine that you are the owner of a nearby fast-food restaurant who does a good business at Christmastime because of the increased number of visitors to the area. Write your name on the line in step 1 on page 112. Then follow the instructions there.

Communication Activity 31

Here are some of the puzzle clues. Do not show this to the other students in your group. You may read and discuss the clues.

1 down: The earth is one of these	2 across: a famous woman leader
4 down: He came from a different planet	5 down: a country in Europe
7 down: word before egg or umbrella	8 across: sounds like a number
11 down: a choice	13 across: a continent
18 across: When you cook it, it gets slimy	19 down: a preposition used with time
21 across: Is the moon square?	22 across: a small number
10 down: He liked to drink something special	
14 down: Some people like it; some people hate it	
16 down: the first name of a former international airline	
16 across: Solidarity was born here	

Communication Activity 32

Write this line on page 37: Just before landing, the pilots decided to abort the landing and try again.

Communication Activity 33

Here are some of the puzzle clues. Do not show this to the other students in your group. You may read and discuss the clues.

17 across: a form of *to be*	2 down: meat from a cow
6 across: a kind of bird	5 down: a color
20 down: what aliens get around in	4 across: where pork comes from
7 down: the biggest city in the United Kingdom	18 down: I love her. She loves —.
12 down: the same —	16 down: it divides Panama in two
10 across: what the "price of a sweater" and the "name of that book" have in common	11 across: Japanese have two, Americans have three, and Latin Americans have four or more, but most pets only have one

Communication Activity 34

1. *Don't bite the hand that feeds you.* The analogy is that if you are feeding a cat or dog and the animal suddenly bites you, you will stop feeding it. If someone is helping you, you shouldn't complain about the person or the help. If you complain, then the person who is helping you (feeding you) might stop helping you altogether.
2. *Don't cry over spilled milk.* Spilling milk represents a mistake or problem that has occurred. Once the problem happens, it is impossible to change the situation, just as it is impossible to put the milk back into the glass after it has spilled. Thus, this proverb means that you should not worry about mistakes or bad things that have already happened, because you cannot change the past. Instead, think about things that can be changed in the future.

Communication Activity 35

Write this line on page 37: I wanted to calm him down, so I said, "Don't worry. The pilots know what they are doing."

Communication Activity 36

Write this line on page 76: About 15 minutes later, she brought him his order.

Communication Activity 37

Write this line on page 66: The doctor answered, "None."

Communication Activity 38

You support gun control. Your main reason for this support is the unbelievable number of gun-related killings each year. There are just too many guns out there and we need to cut down on the number of guns in order to cut down on the killings.

Communication Activity 39

Write this line on page 37: We were nearing our destination, so the flight attendants came around to get all the cups and to check passengers' seat belts.

Communication Activity 40

1. *Haste makes waste.* This proverb means that you should take your time when planning or doing something. If you do it too quickly, this increases the chances that you might make some mistake that might ruin the thing you are doing or making. For example, A wrote a paper and turned it in without checking for spelling or grammar mistakes. The teacher gave the paper a failing grade and wrote "Haste makes waste" on the paper. This means that A should have spent more time on the paper. A should not have rushed the job.
2. *Every cloud has a silver lining.* A cloud represents something not good, something that might prevent us from accomplishing our goal. However, even a very dark, ominous cloud has a silver edge (or lining). This proverb means that good things can result even from things that are apparently bad. For example, when A was worried because her company was laying off people, she started reading the classified section of the paper; now she has found a much better job. When A tells B that her company might be laying off people, B says, "That's too bad." A replies, "Well, not really. Every cloud has a silver lining. I didn't get laid off, but I did find a much better job."

Communication Activity 41

Write this line on page 76: When they came inside, they walked over to the truck driver's table. One of them took what was left of the burger, and the other one took the cup of coffee.

Communication Activity 42

Here are some of the puzzle clues. Do not show this to the other students in your group. You may read and discuss the clues.

1 across: playing-card suit	7 down: a large city in England
3 down: not happy	19 across: a shortened name for Susan
24 across: a kind of board game	13 down: a river in South America
11 across: you find it on an I.D.	24 across: when one company dominates
18 down: first-person object of a verb or preposition	8 across: finished
13 across: a disease	23 down: the opposite of down

Communication Activity 43

Mrs. Burke was pregnant. Though she felt contractions the night before, she did not really pay any attention to them because the baby wasn't due for another month. The next morning she tried to get a substitute, but it was too late. Her contractions were getting closer. She had her students use the intercom to tell the school office and nurse to call 911, the emergency number. When the paramedics arrived, Mrs. Burke was already in labor, so they delivered the baby in the classroom. The children were cleared from the room before the actual delivery, but one student said the teacher was "white as the sheets." The students were worried because the teacher was obviously in pain.

Communication Activity 44

Write this line on page 37: Then the captain announced, "Ladies and gentlemen, everything is OK. We will be landing on our next attempt. There is nothing to worry about."

Communication Activity 45

Write this line on page 76: "He isn't such a good driver either," she replied. "He just ran over two motorcycles in the parking lot."

Communication Activity 46

1. *Two wrongs do not make a right.* A good friend accidentally forgot your birthday and didn't give you a gift, so on your friend's birthday, you intentionally don't buy a gift for him. This "tit for tat" action is not only childish but simply wrong. It was wrong of your friend to forget your birthday, but ignoring his birthday as an act of revenge doesn't make the situation better. Two wrongs do not make a right.

2. *An ounce of prevention is worth a pound of cure.* This proverb has nothing to do with weights (ounce and pound). It is important to know that an ounce is a very small amount when compared to a pound. This proverb means that it takes much less effort to *prevent* a problem than to solve a problem or undo a mistake. For example, suppose I'm going to the bank to cash a check, and I don't have much time. When I get into my car, I suddenly realize that I don't have my bank card with me. I rarely need it, but sometimes the teller asks me for it. Should I just drive to the bank and hope that the teller won't ask me for the card or should I go back in the house to get it now? I decide to get my card, which takes me about two extra minutes. If I go to the bank without my card and the

teller asks me for it, then I won't be able to cash my check today because I don't have enough time to go to the bank, come home to get my card, and get back to the bank before they close. So in this case, I decide to do the safe thing by getting my card now. Thus, an ounce of prevention is worth a pound of cure.

Communication Activity 47

Write this line on page 66: He said, "I'm worried about my weight."

Communication Activity 48

Imagine that you are a parent who brings his/her children to see the Osbornes' beautiful Christmas display every year. Write your name on the line in step 1 on page 112. Then follow the instructions there.

Communication Activity 49

Write this line on page 76: The waitress went to his table and asked him for his order.

Communication Activity 50

You are definitely opposed to gun control. Your 26-year-old brother was shot and killed in a robbery attempt just outside your house last year. The robbers had a gun, and now you want a gun. If they come back, you want to be ready.

Communication Activity 51

Here are some of the puzzle clues. Do not show this to the other students in your group. You may read and discuss the clues.

2 across: a former British prime minister
3 down: Pete Sampras's sport
5 down: Its capital is Bucharest.
6 across: abbreviation for Los Angeles
9 across: the opposite of *from*
8 across: a connector word
12 down: a fish movie
15 across: a continent
16 down: similar to a pot
17 down: abbreviation for *don't know*
19 down: a preposition used with places
20 down: a verb used with *the laundry*
22 across: the smallest even number
11 down: similar to -ist (dent*ist*) or -er (teach*er*)
14 down: It appears in some places in the winter.

Communication Activity 52

There is no doubt that a less experienced pilot could not have landed that flight as well as Captain Haynes was able to do. Even similar simulated flights without hydraulic capabilities crashed. Here is an individual who has certainly demonstrated that his skills are not only up to par but are also far superior to what is required on a daily basis. If we do not trust people to fly a plane after they reach 60, then why do we let those same people drive a car on our streets? Surely by the same line of thinking, we should think that these people might have an auto accident and kill someone. However, that is not what we think. We do not take away people's driver's licenses when they reach 60 or 65 or 70. There should be a better system that would allow capable pilots to continue flying if they wished to do so.

Communication Activity 53

Here is the whole story. The man went to the restroom on the train. He accidentally dropped his identification papers in the toilet. He decided to reach into the toilet to get his papers out, but when he did this, his hand got stuck. No one on the train could get the passenger's hand out of the toilet, so when the train arrived in Tours, specialists were there to help the passenger out of this embarrassing situation. Unfortunately, they could not get his hand out of the toilet, so the toilet had to be cut out of the train car floor and then the man, his arm still in the toilet, was taken to the hospital.

Communication Activity 54

Imagine that you work for the city tourist office. Write your name on the line in step 1 on page 112. Then follow the instructions there.

Communication Activity 55

Write this line on page 76: He was such a big, strong man that the people in the cafe couldn't help noticing him when he first came in.

Decisions in Court Cases

Exercise 1.3

Even though the new job had the same salary, the same benefits, and the same office as before, a Wisconsin court ruled that the jobs were not equivalent because Marquardt's "authority and responsibility were greatly reduced in the new position." After the court ordered another hearing to determine back salary, the two parties settled out of court for an undisclosed amount.

Exercise 2.4

The judge rejected the lawsuit by Mr. Deskiewicz, Jr. His reason for doing this did not involve whether or not Philip Morris was responsible for the nicotine addiction. The judge said that the three-year statute of limitations had expired since Mr. Deskiewicz had first tried to quit in 1971.

Exercise 2.10

The judge ruled that Susan Tanner's smoking was endangering Elysa's health. The judge gave temporary custody of Elysa to Steven Masone's mother.

Exercise 6.5

The first courts, which were in Iowa, ruled that the Schmidts should have custody of Jessica, since Dan had not signed away his parental rights. The DeBoers appealed this decision and eventually the case reached the Iowa State Supreme Court, which again ruled that the biological parents should have custody of Jessica for the same reason. Iowa law states that biological parents have custodial rights unless a child has been abandoned—which Dan had not done—and only in the case of abandonment can the court consider the child's rights over the biological parents' rights.

The DeBoers appealed this decision in a Michigan court. The Michigan Circuit Court ruled that Jessica should stay with the DeBoers because she might never get over losing the only parents she had ever known. Clearly the court was concerned about Jessica's welfare. The judge said he understood the Schmidt's pain in his decision but explained that "prolonging this battle is going to have a terrible effect on this child." The judge said the Schmidts would be true heroes if they made this sacrifice (of their parental rights) for Jessica.

Not wanting to give up, the Schmidts appealed to a higher court in Michigan. A few months later, the Michigan State Supreme Court ruled 6–1 that the state of Michigan had no jurisdiction over the case and that Jessica would have to be returned to the Schmidts in a month.

This case sparked an outcry across the United States. In a poll in *Glamour* magazine (January 1994), 87 percent of respondents said the court was wrong to send Jessica DeBoer back to the Schmidts. When asked who was most at fault for this case, 33 percent said the courts for allowing this case to last so long, 31 percent said Cara Schmidt for lying about the birth father, 31 percent said both the Schmidts for trying to uproot Jessica, and only 5 percent said the DeBoers for dragging on a case that they knew they legally had no chance of winning. What do you think?

Exercise 6.8

The judge said that if a minor in the state of Florida can choose abortion, "then surely a minor child has the right to assert a constitutional privilege to resist an attempt to remove her from the only home she has known. . . and declare her the child of strangers."

Kimberly's lawyer said, "She has lived in fear for five years of being taken from her father in the name of her so-called biological parents. The problem is that we've defined parenthood in terms of biology. That's a myth. Once a child is nurtured and cared for, you've got a family."

Exercise 6.11

The judge decided to award custody to Kay, Tyler's grandmother. The judge cited a 1985 Virginia State Supreme Court ruling that a parent's homosexuality was grounds for having custody of a child taken away because of the state's anti-homosexual laws.

Sharon appealed the case to the next highest court. The three judges for the Virginia Court of Appeals overturned the first court's decision and awarded custody back to Sharon. A judge on the appeals court wrote, "The social science evidence showed that a person's sexual orientation does not strongly correlate with that person's fitness as a parent. A parent's private sexual conduct, even if illegal, does not create a presumption of unfitness." Tyler's grandmother appealed the case to the next highest court.

The Virginia State Supreme Court ruled 4–3 in favor of Tyler's grandmother. The court said that Sharon Bottoms was an unfit parent and that it was in the best interest of Tyler to be with his grandmother. Ironically, the court explained its decision by stating that Tyler would face discrimination from society if he lived with his mother and her lover.

Tyler is currently living with his grandmother. It is not clear whether Sharon Bottoms will appeal this decision, nor is it clear whether the Supreme Court would agree to hear this case. Until a final decision is reached (when neither party appeals again or when the case reaches the U.S. Supreme Court, whichever comes first), the ruling that Tyler be with his grandmother is valid.

In a related event, the highest court in New York has ruled that unmarried people—gay or straight—have a right to adobt their partners' children. New York has a law that says that any qualified individual—gay or straight—can adopt, so this recent ruling was an extension of a previous law. Chief Judge Judith Kaye wrote: "To rule otherwise would mean that the thousands of New York children actually being raised in homes headed by two unmarried persons could only have one legal parent, not the two who want them."

By allowing unmarried partners to adopt, the court can guarantee that the children receive a range of financial benefits that are now in question.

Exercise 21.6

On May 23, 1994, the jury acquitted Rodney Peairs of manslaughter but ordered him to pay $653,000 to the Hattoris. Peairs's lawyer stated in his closing argument, "You have the absolute right in this country to answer your door with a gun." In many states, his statement is technically correct. (You should realize that gun laws, like many laws in the United States, do vary greatly from state to state. Louisiana gun laws are not as strict as in some other states.)

When the news came out, people in Japan reacted with anger and disbelief to Peairs's acquittal. It is hard for Americans to understand how rare shootings are in Japan; ownership of most weapons is not allowed. In 1991, for example, only 74 people in all of Japan died of gunshot wounds, and 67 of those people were connected to organized crime. In the United States, which has about double the population, more than 24,000 were killed in the same year. (For comparison, in 1990 the United Kingdom reported 22 gun fatalities and Sweden had only 13.)

Yoshihiro's father attended all seven days of the trial. Afterwards, he said that the jury's verdict was "unbelievable." He added, "I don't believe this verdict represents the rest of this country." Mr. Hattori and his wife led a petition campaign to get signatures of people who wanted to eliminate handguns in the United States. Eventually, they were able to present their petition of 1.6 million signatures in person to President Bill Clinton. Unfortunately, the handgun problem persists.

The Hattoris realize that they may never get all of the money awarded them in this case, but they do want to get one thing: they want the gun that killed their son Yoshihiro to be destroyed.

Japanese journalist Hirochi Sekiguchi, covering Peairs' trial, said, "Many Japanese people cannot believe why the United States allows its people to have guns. A gun is a weapon to kill other people, we believe."

Exercise 22.6

The industrial tribunal also found that McParland was unfairly fired. However, the tribunal ruled that McParland himself was partly responsible for his dismissal and reduced the amount of the compensation by one-third, to $1,350.

Exercise 24.3

The case went all the way to the Arkansas State Supreme Court. The Court ruled that the Osbornes should cut back on their display in order to reduce the large crowds. A lower court had ruled that the Osbornes keep the lights on for only 15 days, hire guards, set up trash barrels, and post no-littering signs. Mr. Osborne was not happy with the decision, claiming that it violated his right to free speech and religious expression. There is a possibility that he might try to appeal to the U.S. Supreme Court.

Exercise 25.3

At the current time, the case is still pending. Students should discuss what they think the judge should decide.

Exercise 26.17

The case generated a great deal of publicity. Many people were outraged that the judicial system, which is already filled with too many cases involving much more important issues, was being further clogged up with such a frivolous case as this one. The prosecutor decided to drop the case, so Mr. Balun did not have to pay any fines or serve any time in jail. However, since the cruelty to animal law in the state does not specifically mention rats as an exception, it is theoretically possible for someone else to find himself in the same legal trouble that Mr. Balun was in if he killed a rat in a cruel way.

Exercise 28.11

Officer Meinhold announced his homosexuality on television in May 1994 and received his discharge in August. On November 6, 1994, Judge Terry Hatter, Jr., ordered the navy to reinstate Meinhold while the case was being resolved. On November 12, Officer Meinhold was sworn back into military service, thus becoming the first openly gay man to be reinstated into the military as a result of a court challenge. The navy did not contest the decision within the allotted time, and Officer Meinhold was able to serve in the navy again without fear of being expelled because of his sexual orientation.

Exercise 31.3

The jury cleared Dr. Kevorkian of the murder charges. They said that the patient had "a right to die" with dignity. One juror said, "I don't feel it's our obligation to choose for someone else how much pain and suffering they can go through. . . . I feel each person should be able to make their own choice." There are currently 30 states with laws against medicides. It remains to be seen when, if ever, these laws will be changed.

Exercise 31.12

The judge ruled that Benny was old enough to make his own decision about this matter and that Benny was fully aware of all the consequences of this decision. Benny spent the last months of his life playing video games with friends and watching his tropical fish. He died on September 5, 1994.

Answer Key for Language Review Exercises

Unit 1, p. 2: 1. c 2. a 3. b 4. b 5. b 6. c 7. a 8. a 9. b 10. a

Unit 2, p. 10: 1. severe 2. expose 3. addictive 4. policy 5. custody 6. sued (*or* is suing) 7. appropriate 8. covers 9. aggravated 10. ended up

Unit 3, pp. 12–13: 1. clarify 2. familiar with 3. recount 4. maximum 5. keep me in mind 6. systematic 7. clarification 8. plot 9. minimum 10. character

Unit 4, p. 17: 1. executed 2. barred 3. quarters 4. likely 5. strict (*or* stricter) 6. arranged 7. discontinued (*or* has discontinued, will discontinue, is discontinuing) 8. raced 9. all at once 10. Currently 11. brought about 12. bullets

Unit 5, pp. 20–21: 1. occurred 2. get it out (*or* get it out of your thumb) 3. does the weather (*or* the cold weather, that) have to do with 4. on my own 5. is (*or* has gotten) stuck 6. recently 7. has to do with 8. got (*or* is) stuck

Unit 6, pp. 27–28: 1. c 2. b 3. c 4. a 5. b 6. a 7. c 8. b 9. a 10. c 11. b 12. a 13. a 14. c 15. b 16. c 17. b 18. a 19. a 20. c 21. b 22. b 23. a 24. c 25. b

Unit 7, pp. 32–33: 1. fails 2. premature 3. will 4. laying off 5. spoil 6. in charge of 7. content 8. put off 9. accomplished 10. ominous

Unit 8, p. 36: 1. a 2. b 3. c 4. b 5. a 6. c 7. c

Unit 9, p. 38: 1. f 2. d 3. b 4. a 5. c 6. e 7. g

Unit 10, p. 46: 1. b 2. a 3. c 4. c 5. a 6. b 7. a 8. a 9. c 10. b 11. a 12. b 13. c 14. a 15. c

Unit 11, pp. 48–49: 1. prepositions 2. laundry 3. jaws 4. continent 5. planet 6. Okra 7. geography 8. abbreviation 9. crisis 10. site

Unit 12, p. 53: 1. a 2. a 3. b 4. c 5. b 6. a 7. a 8. b 9. b 10. a 11. c 12. a

Unit 13, p. 57: (These are possible answers; students' answers will vary.) 1. they are both brown, they are both drinks, people usually drink them hot, you can put milk in both of them, they both have caffeine 2. they are both countries, they are both in South America, they both have good football (soccer) teams, they both end in the letter *a*, they both have produced many fine writers 3. *various* 4. *various*

Unit 14, pp. 64–65: 1. entire 2. resume 3. impact 4. shudder 5. mandatory 6. dip 7. crack 8. take a chance 9. went out 10. wreckage 11. stamina 12. initial 13. retire 14. remarkable 15. odds

Unit 15, pp. 66–67: 1. d 2. a 3. f 4. e 5. g 6. b 7. c

Unit 16, pp. 74–75: 1. sentence; fine 2. cut down on; eliminate 3. cited 4. plays (*or* played, has played) a role; homicides 5. typical; era 6. broke into 7. the bottom line 8. launching

Unit 17, p. 77: 1. 35 2. three 3. (*various*) apples, pears 4. *various* 5. *various*

Unit 18, p. 82: 1. a 2. a 3. c 4. b 5. b 6. c 7. c 8. c 9. b 10. b

Unit 19, p. 89: 1. set up 2. persistent 3. emphasize 4. exchanged (*or* have exchanged, will exchange, am exchanging) 5. fluid 6. violated 7. come up with 8. deserved 9. spread 10. effective

Unit 20, pp. 91–92: 1. *various* 2. Mr. Chavez 3. (*various*) instant potatoes, a hot dog 4. (*various*) a stop sign 5. (*various*) a hospital, a school, a big home, an office 6. *various*

Unit 21, pp. 98–99: 1. dressed up as; costume 2. inhabit 3. security 4. took place 5. released 6. regulates 7. stark 8. attach 9. by mistake 10. imitation 11. cut down on; smuggling 12. fired

Unit 22, pp. 102–3 1. the norm 2. promptly 3. insult 4. remark 5. circumstances 6. globe 7. deliberately 8. dismissed 9. grievances 10. compensation

Unit 23, p. 109: 1. *various* 2. *various* 3. et cetera; incorporated; AIDS awareness 4. *various* 5. *various* 6. *various*

Unit 24, pp. 112–13: 1. d 2. f 3. i 4. h 5. a 6. e 7. b 8. j 9. g 10. c

Unit 25, p. 116: 1. c 2. b 3. a 4. b 5. c 6. a 7. b 8. a

Unit 26, pp. 125–26: 1. Practically 2. option 3. makes up; pace 4. roamed
5. evaluate 6. Halt 7. fate 8. wiggle 9. relieved 10. Due to 11. boils down to
12. slaughtered 13. devastating 14. stabilize

Unit 27, p. 132: *various*

Unit 28, pp. 140–41: 1. opposed; partnership 2. kicked out of 3. have nothing to
do with 4. discrimination; come out 5. submissive 6. adhere to 7. controversial *or*
heated 8. adultery 9. phobia 10. pertains to

Unit 29, pp. 143–44: 1. yolk; ingredients 2. strategy; quantity 3. dominated
4. role; fatal 5. vanish

Unit 30, p. 147: 1. routine; counter 2. stack; turn in 3. stray 4. reward

Unit 31, pp. 154–55: Part A: 1. Former; passed away 2. joints 3. will 4. consequences 5. In case 6. rejected (*or* has rejected, is rejecting, will reject) 7. prolong
8. irritable Part B: 1. b 2. a 3. c 4. a 5. b 6. c 7. a 8. b 9. a 10. c 11. c 12. b

Unit 32, p. 159: 1. m 2. i 3. l 4. f 5. n 6. c 7. a 8. k 9. b 10. d 11. j 12. h
13. e 14. g